Light Your FIRE

Financial Independence and Retire Early -
The Complete Guide

Mark Davies

Uranus Publishing

Light Your Fire

Contents

INTRODUCTION

L et's start with a question: Why do we spend our whole lives working for someone else and never truly living the lives we want to? We've been taught that this is just the way life is. We've seen our parents do it, and they have seen their parents do it. It just seems like all life is cracked up to be, right? Wrong! Just because we have seen generations do this before us does not mean that is how it has to be. We have other options now, and we should be at the forefront trying to take advantage of them. We have access to knowledge that those before us did not have, which means that we can live differently.

Now, don't get me wrong. We should be thankful for the sacrifices our parents and grandparents made so that we could have a better life. We shouldn't force ourselves into that way of life if there is a better option. The good news is that there is a better option. There is a way for you to get to a point where you can live the life you want to live. A life where working is an option and doing the things you love becomes a priority in your everyday life. All you need is the right blueprint, and that blueprint has been provided for us through the FIRE movement.

FIRE stands for "Financial Independence, Retire Early," and it really does just say what it means. This movement is about reaching financial independence to not live your life just in a continuous cycle of working to have money to live. It's about being able to retire early, hang up your work boots, and trade them in for a pair of comfy slippers, if you so desire. It is really about being able to dictate what you want your everyday life to look like. It's not a pie in the sky theory; it is actually a way of life that many people have adopted, worked toward, and achieved.

It is no secret that the COVID-19 pandemic has shifted our lives' perspective. Our worlds have changed in a blink of an eye. Jobs are not stable, and suddenly we are not allowed to move around and travel. The things that we planned on doing are no longer possible.

However, there has been some good that has come out of this. More than ever, people have realized what is important in life. Spending time with those you love and not pushing off things until later have become priorities. Work has also changed. More opportunities to work from home and create an online income have arisen. How we earn money and how we live has changed, and it has created the perfect mindset to pursue financial independence.

Before we move on any further, I want to clarify that what I am talking about is not a scheme that claims to get you rich as quickly as possible with the least amount of work. FIRE is not about getting rich; it is about being free. There is more to life than money, and that more is what we are going to be focused on getting: The things that make life fulfilling and worth living.

If you didn't have to work a day in your life, what would your days consist of? Traveling to new and exciting places? Living off the grid in a small cottage somewhere? Spending time with your family and watching your kids grow up? Whatever your answer is, that is what you will be working toward. Some people still choose to work once they have reached financial independence, the difference being that they can work for pleasure and do something they love. That is what financial independence can provide you with: True freedom.

I'm not going to give you the "you can do whatever you put your mind to" speech because you will need a little more than just a winning mindset. You will need the right knowledge, and then you have to take that knowledge and apply it to reach your goals of financial independence. That is what this book provides. It gives you the right knowledge, steps, and tools to reach the goal of financial independence.

By the time you reach the end of this book, you will have learned how to aggressively save so that you can live the way you want to later. You will be able to pick out the things in your life that you need to change, and you will have a shift in perspective on what life is truly about.

Chapter 1

F.I.R.E. EXPLAINED

F irst of all, no, FIRE is not about setting all your money on fire and hoping for the best. It is a movement that is geared to helping people find financial freedom. FIRE has gained popularity among younger people who have not yet reached retirement age.

The goal is to accumulate enough money, through assets, to retire as early as possible. Your first target is to save 50% to 70% of your total income and then live off the rest until you have enough to retire. Aggressively saving is what allows the devotees of this movement to retire early. Usually, the timeline is about ten years from the day you start saving and investing.

To most people, that sounds crazy. I mean, people spend the years from their early 20s all the way up to their 60s saving for retirement, and now people are claiming to be able to do it in a span of 10 years. The thing is, people have done it, and there are more and more people who are retiring earlier than what is expected.

FIRE is not about getting rich quick or making all the money in the world. It is about learning to manage the money that you do have well so that you get to enjoy your life. A majority of the people who attain FIRE are not millionaires by the age of 30. They are normal middle-class workers who have learned the tricks to be free from financial constraints. So the good news is that most people will be able to implement some level of FIRE in their lives.

How It All Started

While the FIRE movement is a fairly new one, the premise of financial independence has been around for a while. It all started in 1992 with Vicki Robin and Joe Dominguez. That was the year they published their book, *Your Money or Your Life,* which spoke about the idea of financial independence as the alternative to spending the best years of your life working at a 9-to-5 to make your money.

Joe Dominguez retired at the age of 31 after working a job on Wall Street. So this premise was not just an idea; it was their way of life. Vicki and Joe did not start the FIRE movement, but they have been sourced as the inspiration for it. The way they lived and their book's principles were the starting point of this movement.

Twenty-five years later, the FIRE movement began to take shape. People started seeing their parents making it to 65 and not having the amazing retirement that had been sold to them. Consumerism and keeping up with the Joneses were ruining their financial futures. Out of this came FIRE, and it grew into the movement it is now. Many bloggers, podcasters, and writers jumped on the bandwagon and started educating others on this new way of life.

Reasons to Pursue Financial Independence

There are plenty of reasons to pursue financial freedom. It does not have to be about retiring early to live off the grid in a villa somewhere in Spain. Freedom is freedom, and it means that you get to do whatever you want with your life, and that is what people are chasing after. Once you have attained that freedom, your life is yours to do with what you wish. Now, we're going to discuss the reasons why I feel that everyone should chase financial independence.

<u>You Have the Freedom to Do Something You Enjoy</u>

For many people, the FIRE movement is not about retiring and just relaxing for the rest of their life. Many people still want to work, but they want to do something they love, and that gives them a sense of purpose. The only problem with this is that many fulfilling jobs and passions don't pay the bills, or at least they won't at first.

When you have financial independence, it doesn't matter if you earn a lot of money from your job because your financial needs are already taken care of. Finances and stability are what drive people into careers and companies, even if they have no passion for the work they are doing. Once you are financially secure, nothing stops you from quitting your job and chasing after something you have always wanted to do. Even if you don't know where your passion lies, you have the freedom to take your time and discover them.

You no longer have to be stuck in a boring office job if your passion is wildlife and conservation. You don't have to work in marketing if you have always dreamed of opening your own camp or center for kids. You can even finally go back to school and study something you enjoy if you want to switch your career path. More and more people want to be doing things that are meaningful with their lives, and FIRE provides an opportunity to pursue that.

You Get to Spend More Time With Your Family

Life is short, and we only get a little while to spend with the people we love. Hectic work schedules and long hours shorten that time even more. We always hear parents saying how quickly their children grew up and children saying they wished they could spend more time with their elderly parents. Having more time to spend with those we cherish is the number one wish of so many people.

When you are no longer bound by a strict work schedule or having to put in overtime to make ends meet, your time is freed up to be with your family. You don't have to miss important moments because there is an emergency at work or because you have an unreasonable boss who wants you to spend a majority of your time catering to their needs.

You can be there for your kids, watch their sports games, and help them with their homework. If you have an elderly parent, you can help take care of them or just spend time with them. Family ties will become stronger, and you will eventually have a more fulfilling life enriched with precious moments.

You Get to Travel More

Many people in the workforce only get about ten days of paid vacation per year. Worse still, some people don't get any paid vacation days. This means that the workforce is filled with people who are burning out and have no time to enjoy their lives. A majority of people want to travel, see the world, and go on vacation, but it is just not possible with certain working situations.

When you have financial independence, you can book a flight to Mexico today if that is what you want. Taking a three-week-long safari trip to Africa does not have to be something that just sits on your bucket list for years and years; it can become a reality. Most people want to see the world and travel to new places. There is so much to see and explore that it is no surprise that traveling has become one of this generation's top goals.

Traveling is not only good for holidays, but it also expands your mind. You get to see how other people live and explore different cultures. Well-traveled people tend to be much more sympathetic to issues facing other parts of the world, and they have a broader perspective on global issues. This kind of insight can open your eyes and help you to think differently in your own life. Even traveling around your own country can be eye-opening and fun. You never know what you have right outside your doorstep until you actually step out and find it.

You Can Pick Up and Move or Become Location Independent

Being financially independent opens up a whole new world of opportunities for you. You can literally pick up and leave to go and live anywhere in the world if that is what you desire. You don't have to stay in the big city because that is where the job opportunities are. These kinds of restraints are no longer on you. Whether you want to take a sabbatical to live off the grid in a hut in the Maldives or just move closer to your family, you have the option to do so.

Many central, big cities are expensive to live in. Think of New York and Los Angeles. These are big cities where many people move to pursue their career goals and make a lot of money. Maybe they do make lots of money, but living in these cities is very expensive.

From rent to groceries, these places often have a much higher cost of living than somewhere like Buffalo, El Paso or Memphis.

In fact, many places all over the world have a far lower cost of living than places in the USA, so you could have a better quality of life at a fraction of the cost. Many people are moving to eastern Europe, South America, and Southeast Asia for this very reason. If it has always been your dream to move somewhere else in the world, then this is your ticket to do so. You don't have to be bound to one location. You could spend every six months in a different country because your income depends not on you going into an office every weekday.

Types of FIRE

Over the years, there have been many FIRE variations that have been developed. This is to include various people and what they are capable of doing. Some don't necessarily want to go full FIRE but still want to implement the movement's principles. It also outlines the lifestyles that the followers want or can abide by.

LeanFIRE

This variation of FIRE focuses on extreme minimalism by emphasizing a lean way of living. Essentially you are saving up as much money as possible in the shortest amount of time. You would retire more modestly, so you are not saving to live a lavish retirement. Due to the intense saving and aiming for a smaller income during retirement, reaching financial independence is archived much sooner than other variations.

If you want to do leanFIRE, you must be ready to live a frugal lifestyle. You will be cutting out most luxuries and only spending money on the things you really need. People who prefer a simple, minimalist lifestyle often choose this variation because they do not aim to have fancy things, big homes, or constant traveling. Often they choose to live in areas that have a lower cost of living to further save money or allow a better quality of life with a smaller budget.

FatFIRE

This variation is still about saving as much as you can, but it has a more insurgent approach. Followers of this method still aim to save a large portion of their income to put toward retirement but do not give up as much as those doing the leanFIRE approach. Their lifestyles reflect a more traditional lifestyle. Thus, it will take longer to reach FIRE and probably require a higher income to save more. If you choose the fatFIRE variation, you can still enjoy the luxuries and extras in life; you will just need to find a way to save more and earn more.

Many people who choose this approach will aim toward a high-paying career or start a side hustle to bring in more money. This way, even if you are saving a large chunk of your income, you can still have a more expensive lifestyle. As with every variation of FIRE, sacrifices need to be made, but they are not as big as the sacrifices made in leanFIRE.

BaristaFIRE

For this, you are still working and saving in order to quit your main job early, but you are not aiming to not work at all. People who follow baristaFIRE want to quit their nine to five but still have some sort of part-time work or a lower-paying job that helps cover certain expenses or can be put back into savings.

This part-time job or lower-income job is usually something that the person is passionate about and finds joy in doing. They are still not ruled by money or whether their job will provide enough for them because they have saved up enough to have the basics covered. The jobs they usually go for have benefits like health insurance. This way, some financial pressure is taken off the person. Working at Starbucks is one of these options, hence the name baristaFIRE.

When you get to work for pleasure rather than obligation, you love what you do. If you no longer want to work in that company or want to try something else, you are free to do so. The money that you earn from your work is not used to cover your expenses but is used to add to your savings or can be used to buy luxuries or pay for experiences. Many people choose baristaFIRE because they still want to work but want to do it on their terms.

CoastFIRE

The goal behind this type of FIRE is to pile as much money as you can into your savings at a young age to reap the benefits of compound interest. The earlier you start, the less money you have to save because you still have many years until the time you want to retire. On the other side of the scale, the older you are when you start, the more money you will need to invest to get the same results.

Essentially you are maximizing time and investment. You will need to work out how much money you would like in retirement and then, from there, work out how much you would need to save. The standard rule for this is the 25x rule. For this, you will need to take the annual amount you want available at retirement and multiply it by 25, and this will show you how much you need in your savings to reach that goal. So if you want $50,000 annually when you retire, you would need a minimum of $1.25 million in a tax-advantaged savings account.

Once you know how much you need to save up, you can work on a plan to reach that goal. The amount you place in the bank account will increase with interest, and you no longer have to contribute to the savings account. For instance, if you can get $100,000 into your savings account, assuming a 95% stock/5% cash portfolio and an 8.1% annual ROI by the age of 30, it would reach $1.3 million by the age of 65. This means that you have reached coastFIRE by age 30 because you can now 'coast' toward financial independence.

With this method, you will reach financial independence quicker than the other methods. However, it is more complicated than the other methods because it does require you to have a very high savings rate early on in your career. This can be difficult for most people since they are still working their way up the career ladder and may not earn enough to save what is required.

If you can implement this method, you should definitely go for it. Just try to make some additional contributions during market downturns; this way, you will make sure that you have enough when the time comes to retire.

Basic Steps to FIRE

Even though there are different variations of FIRE, all of them have some definite steps. The goal is to be able to retire earlier than the average person, and this won't happen unless you know what to do and then do those things properly. We will be talking about each step more in-depth as we progress through the book, but for now, I want to give you an overview so that you know what to expect.

<u>Find Your Motivation</u>

Doing anything in life would be extremely difficult if we didn't have the motivation. It's the light at the end of the tunnel that will keep us going even when we do not want to. Earlier in the chapter, we went through some of the reasons to pursue financial independence. Maybe your motivation is on that list, or maybe it is something completely different. Whatever you are aiming for, that is what has to be at the forefront of your mind as you move through this journey.

Remember, this is not going to happen overnight. You will be getting to financial independence much quicker than most people, but that still does not mean that you will blink and it will be handed to you. Prepare for a good few years of hard work. It is in these times that your motivation will need to kick in. That is why it is essential to determine why you want to go on this journey right from the beginning.

Plan

Before you start anything in life, you need a good plan. You need to know where you are headed to know the right steps and prepare for that. If you have a solid plan, you will be more likely to succeed than if you just wing it and hope for the best. Planning allows you to measure your progress and see if you are on track or if you need to adjust.

Readjusting your plan will be inevitable. There will always be something that comes up or a new piece of information added to the mix. The plan does not have to be so strict that you can never change it, but it does have to provide you with a good outline of what the future will look like and what you have to do to get there.

When you are planning for FIRE, there are some key questions that you have to ask yourself:

- What is my current income?
- What are my expenses currently?
- What is the standard of living that I would be happy to retire in?
- How much will it cost to maintain that standard of living?
- At what age do I want to retire?
- How much do I need to save to retire at the age I want to?
- What am I willing to cut back on?
- What other income sources will I be getting once I retire (part-time job, passive income, pension, etc.)?
- Do I need to increase my income to reach my retirement goals?

Asking yourself these questions will put you on the right track to planning. As you work through the planning stage, you might begin to ask yourself other questions, but just make sure that these have been answered to ensure that you have covered the basics. You will see that some of your answers will clash. For instance, if the savings you need to retire is too much to accumulate over the amount you have until you want to retire, you will have to make a compromise somewhere.

Planning will help you get a realistic view of what you can do versus your expectations. When you plan, make sure you are being specific. Don't just say you want a higher standard of living, make sure to define it for yourself. Write down what you would want your retirement to look like, and then try to link that to numerical figures.

Remember to be realistic. The goal of FIRE is not to live this lavish lifestyle with minimal effort but to sacrifice where you can, so that you will be able to achieve financial freedom.

<u>Spend Less</u>

To save more, you will need to spend less. Many of us don't even realize how much useless stuff we buy until we write it all down. So before you do anything else, you will need to review your monthly and annual spending. See what you spend your money on and what your most significant expenses are.

There will be things on your list that are non-negotiable, like rent, utilities, loans, and perhaps a vehicle. These things usually have a fixed amount that you have to pay per month, so you might not be able to cut back on these things. Other things, like food, clothing, activities, and other luxuries, probably can be cut back on in some way.

Reducing your spending is not just so that you can save, but it will carry you through your retirement as well. If you choose leanFIRE, you will be living a simpler lifestyle. Changing the brands of items you buy to cheaper ones, thrifting, choosing to eat at home rather than at restaurants, and finding cheaper hobbies or things to do on the weekends are all great ways to save some extra money.

Save, Save, Save

As you have probably noticed, saving is a crucial part of FIRE because it is how you will have enough money for retirement. Some of the FIRE savings goals might seem a bit intimidating, but you can start small and build yourself up. The important thing is that you make saving a priority.

Once you have cut back and decided where you can spend less, you will be able to put all of that money into your savings. Saving needs to be your priority and needs to be done before you go out and spend your money. If you leave it until after you have bought everything you want to, you will have very little money to save.

Think of saving as paying yourself, so remember to do this first.

Get Out of Debt

There wouldn't be much of a point in saving if you still have a lot of debt to pay off. To be financially free, you have to be debt-free. Owing money to other people or organizations will keep you bound to them, and that is no form of freedom. The longer you take to handle debt, the worse it can become.

Many people put off dealing with their debt because the reality of it is not an attractive one. Instead of focusing on what your debt is now, focus on how you will feel once you no longer have any of it holding you back. You probably know the debt you have, but you need to get it out on paper in front of you to properly assess the situation. Once you do that, you should get started on a plan of how you will start paying all of it off.

Later on in the book, we will have an in-depth discussion about debt and what you can do to get rid of it so that you can move forward into true financial freedom.

Increase Your Income

When trying to reach your savings goals, there is only so much you actually can save and cut back on. If you want to reach your savings goals quicker, you may want to consider getting another income source or finding a way to increase the income you currently make. This can be done by working harder at your job to get a promotion or finding a second job, or a side hustle.

If you decide to increase your income, just remember not to fall into the lifestyle inflation trap. Often when someone earns more money, they increase their standards of living almost automatically. Regardless of how much more money you make, keep your living standard the same. Otherwise, there wasn't any point in increasing your income.

Invest

When you invest your money, you generate passive income. This is income that you don't have to do anything to get. Creating a source of passive income should be the goal of every person who wants to reach financial independence. If you are not familiar with investing, it is best to speak to a financial advisor who can show you the best investments for you, your goals, and your situation.

Keep Going Until You Get There

Once you have gotten all your ducks in a row, all you will need to do is keep pushing forward. You will have your goal in sight, so you will have to keep working until you get there. Continuously assessing your finances will be vital to reaching your financial freedom goal. If you need to readjust, then do it. If you have fallen off the wagon and veered away from the plan, get back on the course as soon as you can.

The in-between stages are probably the hardest. The part where you have done all the planning and are still super excited for the prospect of financial freedom will have worn off. Now you will be in the stage where you have to just be consistent and stick to the plan you have laid out for yourself. This is when you will need to go back and remember your motivation.

Eventually, saving and this new lifestyle will become second nature to you. It won't feel like an extra effort; it will just become a habit. This will make life a lot easier. So if you ever feel demotivated in the first few months, know that it does not last forever. After a while, you will be so used to this new normal that it will just become a part of your life. Once you reach financial freedom and you can retire the way you want to, you will be so glad you chose to make certain sacrifices earlier on.

Who is FIRE For?

FIRE used to be thought of as only for those that earned a six-figure salary, but it is for anyone who is willing to make the changes necessary to reach financial independence. It doesn't matter what your salary is. What matters is how much of it you can save. If you are earning, say, $50,000 per year but have a low annual household spending and are able to save a lot of your salary, you could reach FIRE.

The amount of money you earn does play a factor. It is easier to save if you are earning a higher income. You have the option to save more by lowering your standard of living. If you have a low income and are barely scraping by, it will be a lot more challenging to reach financial independence. If you are in that situation, you should be finding ways to increase your income.

FIRE is defined more by a mindset than how much money you make. It is for people who want to retire early and are willing to do what they need to get there. If that means cutting down on luxuries, then do it. If it means finding a way to bring in more money so that you can save more, that is what you will need to do.

FIRE is a mindset followed by specific action to help you reach that goal. Anyone can do it if they are willing to take on that mindset.

How Much Do You Need to Be Financially Independent?

The big question is, how do I know how much money I need to be financially independent? This will be different for everyone since everyone's lifestyle is different. Most FIRE advocates say that working toward 25 times your yearly household spend is a safe number to have. I would say bumping it up to 30 times your yearly spend just to account for any unforeseen circumstances that pop up.

You also have to consider that your spending might go up because you will have more free time and will probably want to travel. Do your best to estimate what you would like your yearly household spend to be and work your savings goal from that.

You should be able to draw 4% of your savings every month for your savings to last your entire retirement. The general number that people aim for is somewhere between $1 million to $2 million. This gives them the security to draw out that 4% every month, but it does differ depending on your household spending.

Along with your savings, it is wise to have at least one or two contingencies, such as a house you own and paid off. If something happens, at least you don't have house payments to make. You could also sell and downsize and use the extra money toward whatever emergency took place. These are all for just in case scenarios, but it is always better to be prepared for them.

You can use online calculators that will give you a ballpark figure on what you need to retire based on several factors. If you do use them, I would suggest using a few and seeing if there is a difference in figures. Each one might use a different formula, so you want to be sure that you are getting the most realistic numbers.

Chapter 2

PLAN YOUR RETIREMENT

E ssentially the whole premise of the FIRE movement is to properly plan for your retirement so that you can retire early and enjoy the rest of your life. You are working toward a goal that will allow you to be free from any unnecessary obligations and live the way you want to.

That is the fun part, but first you have to get serious for a moment and go to the planning part.

Creating Your Retirement Plan

When you first start thinking about retirement, it can be overwhelming. Essentially, you are trying to plan out the rest of your life and the resources you will need to sustain yourself. Many people put it off because of this feeling. I don't want you to keep putting it off, so let's break it down into smaller steps.

Take it little by little and just get started. You will see that it starts to get easier, and very soon you will have it all planned out.

It is imperative to have a plan to know where you are going and what you want your future to look like. If you don't have a plan, you will be going at it blindly and will probably not have enough for retirement or not even be able to retire at all. Once you have a solid plan, you can meet the goals you set for yourself and see where you might need to buckle down a bit more.

As you move through the years, you will need to adjust your plan slightly for unexpected situations or new information that has become available. This is completely normal, so remember that whatever plan you make is flexible.

<u>Assess Where You Are</u>

First things first, you need to know where your starting point is. List out all of your accounts and the amount of money you have saved up in there. This includes savings accounts, retirement funds such as a 401(k), investments, and anything else you have money stored away in. Next, you want to remove anything earmarked for emergencies or saved up for a big purchase like a house or a car. This money has already been allocated to something and does not contribute to your retirement fund.

Once you have done this, you will have an accurate view of your starting point. You will know how much you have, so when you figure out how much you need, this amount can be subtracted from that. If you have not started saving for retirement at all, then you will be starting from zero. This is perfectly fine; you just need to know what your starting point is.

Find Your Sources of Income

You want to have a good idea of the sources of income you will have during retirement. It can be from investments, pension plans, or even a part-time job. Knowing how much money will be coming in will give you a good idea of what you will be able to spend during retirement. Once you know how much money will be coming in during retirement, you will know how much you will need to save.

Check your social security benefits as well. Benefits are given based on various criteria, such as how much you have earned during your career, the age you will be taking your benefits, and the length of your work history. You can get an estimate of how much your benefits will be by going onto the government's website and using their retirement benefit estimator.

Write Down Your Retirement Goals

It is definitely one of the most critical aspects of your retirement planning, and it is probably the most fun. You are thinking about what you want to do when you retire, and from there you can estimate your financial needs. It gives you a good idea about what you are saving toward. Some people want to have a more lavish retirement, and others desire a low-cost, simple life once they retire. How much you will need to save will depend on what you want your retirement to look like.

The best way to go about this is to write down what you want every month of your retirement to look like. Do you want to travel? Where are you planning on living? How much will groceries cost? Take the time to properly plan out a typical month and year in your retirement. You will do this just as you plan out your monthly activities and budget in the present, just taking into account a few extras that you want to be able to do when you retire.

Decide Your Desired Retirement Age

Now that you know what you want your retirement to look like, you need to know how long it will take to get there. Usually, at least ten years from the age you are now is an acceptable minimum. It gives you enough time to save up and plan for the future. Of course, this will all be based on how much you currently have saved up and how much you are willing to save in the time frame before retirement. But let's not focus on the money aspect right now, just think about your goal retirement age.

Try to be as realistic as possible. You will indeed not retire in two years if you have absolutely no savings and earn a small salary. Pick a retirement age that seems doable to you. Another big part of retirement planning is to plan out how many years you will be retired for.

Of course, there is no way to know how long you will actually be alive, but you can have a rough estimate. People are living longer now, and life expectancies are continuing to increase. The average life expectancy in the USA in 2018 was 78.5 years. You can use this as a benchmark and maybe add a few years just in case. Subtracting your retirement age from your estimated life expectancy will give you the number of years you will be retired for.

Decide Your Spending Needs During Retirement

Obviously, you will be spending money throughout your retirement. It will require you to set a budget for yourself to make sure that you can finance your spending. You will be spending on things like groceries, living expenses, traveling, and transport. You can start off by planning how much you will need on a monthly basis.

The best way to develop your future budget is to consider how much you spend right now on certain things. Your grocery budget will probably remain very similar if you don't plan on expanding your family in your retirement. It will change if your kids grow up and move out. See how much you spend on groceries now and then adjust it to the number of people living in your house come retirement. If you plan on being more lavish with groceries in retirement, you will have to increase the amount.

You will also have to take into account where you want to live. It will just be an estimate because there is no way of telling the exact amount of rent or housing payments for a place you do not already live in. You can find the estimated cost of housing and living expenses of different cities and countries on the internet. To be safe, be very conservative with this number.

You would rather have too much saved up than too little. Consider travel and things that will not be daily expenses. If travel is something you desire, you will need to factor it in. Think about how many trips you will want to take per year and how much that will cost you. You can get these numbers by fake planning a holiday and then increasing the prices to account for inflation and other unexpected costs.

Also, make sure to think about leisure activities and doctors' bills. Many people forget to factor these two in, but they will undoubtedly be part of your retirement. You will be doing leisure activities, even if it is just building a puzzle at home. It all counts toward your monthly budget. You will also need to be realistic in the fact that doctors' bills and medication are a very real part of getting older. Even if you plan to retire at 35 and are in perfect health, you are guaranteed to age at some point and will need the extra money to make sure that you can take care of your health needs.

When you are doing this, remember to be realistic. It is better to have a larger estimate than one that is super frugal and the bare minimum. If you are unsure what something will cost, try to stick to the more expensive end of the spectrum. For instance, if you are unsure how much you will need for groceries, plan what you usually would and then add a few extra dollars for a buffer.

Is There a Shortfall?

At this point, you have gathered enough information to have

your retirement planned out, and you know how much you will need to reach your retirement goals. Now it is time to put everything together and see if there is any shortfall. You want your accumulated assets to exceed the amount you need to fund your desired retirement lifestyle.

From all the numbers you have worked out at this point, you should know:

- How much you have.
- How much you will need during retirement.
- How many years until you want to retire.

From these three things, you can figure out whether you are on track or not. Take what you need for retirement and subtract what you have. Then work out how much you will need to save to make up the rest in the number of years you have until your desired retirement date. Further, divide this into a monthly savings contribution. Is this number a realistic savings goal?

If it is, great, you can continue to save as you have been doing, and you will reach your goals by the time you want to. If the amount you need to save in the time frame you have set out is impossible, you need to do some reshuffling. If you still want to retire at the age you set for yourself, you will need to find a way to save more money. You can do this by increasing your income or bucking down and cutting down on your spending so that you can funnel that money into your savings. If you cannot do this, your other option is to increase the time until you retire.

This will allow you to have more time to reach your savings goals while still maintaining the lifestyle that you have at the moment.

Estate Planning

This is not something that is covered very much when speaking about FIRE. The goal of FIRE is to retire early and enjoy your life, but if you have other people counting on you, you also need to plan for that. People with children and families need to be even more conscious when it comes to planning their estate. You do not want to put unnecessary expenses and stress on your family when you are gone.

While you are planning your retirement, take some time to get your estate and affairs in order. If you are very young with few responsibilities or financial assets, this may not be necessary. However, as you get older, and if you choose to build a family and gain assets, you will need to start this process. You will need to get in accountants and lawyers to help you with this process. Essentially you are making sure that your estate will be going to the right people should you pass away. If all of this is in order, it means that the people you want to hand over your estate and wealth to will not have to go through lengthy and expensive probate processes.

Don't Forget Health Insurance

This is something that is often forgotten when people plan to retire early. You usually will not receive federal health insurance until you reach the age of 65. Once you leave your job, you won't be covered by your employer anymore. Let's say you leave your job at the age of 50. That leaves you with 15 years where you won't be covered by health insurance. A lot can happen in those 15 years, and you don't want to take that risk because it might be a costly one if there is a medical emergency that pops up.

You will need to have a plan to bridge the gap between the time you retire and the time the government health insurance kicks in. Every health care plan will be different, and they might vary in different areas. You will have to research the options available to you in your state and see which is the most affordable and full-coverage plan. Remember that health insurance premiums will be more expensive than when you were working at your job. Employers usually cover many costs, and now you will be paying for it on your own. Whatever the number is, it needs to be factored into your retirement budget.

Talk to a Financial Advisor

If you are unsure about anything spoken about or would just rather have someone else manage your finances, it is advisable to get a financial advisor. A good advisor will make sure that your retirement portfolio performs at an optimum level with risk-appropriate asset allocation. This means that you will have a lower chance of losing out if market downturns or anything unexpected happens. It definitely does help to have someone reliable handling your portfolio.

Please take the time to pick out a good financial planner. If you have to try various ones, then do that. Weigh up your options. It is generally better to get a financial advisor who gets paid based on the size of the portfolio they are handling rather than one who gets commission from the products they sell. This way, you can be sure that the person handling your portfolio will want to see it grow and give you the best advice instead of just trying to make a sale.

Talk to Your Significant Other

If you are married or in a long-term relationship, you need to make sure that both of you are on the same page regarding everything we just covered. It is improbable that you will agree on everything, so just planning by yourself can cause some issues down the road. If you both have different ideas on what you want retirement to look like, you will have to talk and come to a compromise before moving forward.

After retirement, couples often do not have the same idea of how they want to spend their time. Almost 50% disagree on how much they need to save to maintain their desired standard of living, and that is from the couples that actually agree on the standard of living they want in retirement (Coxwell, 2020). The only way to avoid entering retirement and finding out that both of you had completely different ideas is to have an honest conversation in the planning stages.

Make sure you talk about where you want to live, how much you want to spend, how you would like to spend your money, and what you want your retirement to look like. Compromise where necessary and work on a plan that will help both of you get the retirement you want.

Change the way you think about money

The most significant aspects of your financial life are not your bank account, investment strategy, or credit score. Your net worth isn't even the most important factor. Your mindset is the most crucial aspect of your financial life.

Those other performance criteria are meaningless unless you have the correct way of thinking and feeling about your financial well-being. A positive mentality leads to positive habits and a positive relationship with money. Without this fundamental approach to financial management, all the great planning and execution in the world will not improve your entire life. Having the proper money mindset entails:

Forming an abundance mindset

Much of the world lives in a scarcity mindset. Scarcity is at the root of the financial crisis, global warfare, and fear-based media. They believe that your good fortune is in jeopardy since the opportunity is limited. A mindset of abundance accepts these dangers but recognizes that there will be additional chances if you plan and execute wisely. Adopting an abundance mindset is what brings the good things in life, so be sure that more good awaits those who plan and act correctly to achieve their objectives.

A smart strategy to develop your abundant mindset is to reframe any intruding, negative thoughts that occur when you are anxious as wonderful opportunities rather than threats.

Anticipating your nature

Knowing yourself and being honest about who you are is an essential part of having a good financial mentality. We are all impulsive, emotional, and messy people. Creating extremely strict budgets that don't allow for your odd urge can derail all of your attempts to better your financial situation. Deprivation can cause you to lash out and hate your efforts in impulsive ways, resulting in overcharges and other unpleasant effects.

Know what your impulsive vices are and make plans to eliminate them in healthy ways while still rewarding yourself on occasion. Whether it's an impulsive purchase of a discounted ebook or a once-a-month trip to the movies, you must allow yourself to enjoy life while working toward financial wellness.

Coping with adversities

Success is never a straight line, and neither is your financial trend line. Changing your habits, investing, and attempting to improve your financial situation all have dangers. Can you live with negative returns on higher-risk investments? Can you manage your money like a business and accept that your money will be working for you in multiple places? Accepting the ongoing existence of change and uncertainty while maintaining confidence in your strategy's ability to work for you is critical for your attitude.

Automated investment and savings solutions can help you with this by keeping it out of sight and out of mind. Market downturns and setbacks are unavoidable, but the key is to remain confident in your excellent approach in the face of market turbulence, which might affect your investments.

Keeping focused

Staying in the process and focusing on the positive outcomes you're aiming for is simple early on in your financial journey. Can you keep that focus throughout the year? What, five years? Figuring out what steps you need to take to stay motivated and work toward financial success is critical for your path. It's a moving target that necessitates brutal honesty with oneself, but staying motivated is critical. Some people utilize vision boards or other simple reminders of their goals.

Some people keep note of their behavior patterns on a calendar or via a smartphone app. What works best for you will not work for everyone else; you simply need to figure out how to keep yourself motivated naturally and efficiently.

Expressing gratitude

Being grateful for what you have now and for the future you are constructing will be highly beneficial. Too many people live their lives negatively and jaded, resenting their existing situation but doing little to change it. It extends beyond simply appreciating what you have. Genuine appreciation entails appreciating the good fortunes of others and contributing to a better world via self-improvement. You are your most important asset, and you should be grateful for the commitment you are making to yourself and your life as you embark on this journey to a better financial life.

Chapter 3

GET RID OF DEBT

Before you even think about saving for FIRE, you must get out of debt. Debt increases the longer you have it, so it is counterproductive to saving. Chances are your debt will compound much faster than you are able to save. Even if you do have a high savings rate, the inevitable truth is that you will need to pay off your debt before you can be financially free.

How to Get Out of Debt

People often ignore their debt because it seems overwhelming to even acknowledge it. No matter how much debt you have, it can be paid off. I won't lie to you, it will take some hard work, but it is definitely possible. The following tips will help you get out of debt and get onto saving for FIRE as soon as possible.

Confront Your Debt

You will never be able to quickly pay off your debt if you don't actually know how much you are paying off. Sometimes it can be scary to come face to face with how much debt you have, especially if you have never kept track of it, but it is necessary for you to do if you want to move forward. Just making the minimum payments and calling it a day isn't going to help you achieve your financial freedom goals.

Start by tallying up all your debt. That includes your car loan, student loan, credit cards, and store cards. See how much your total debt is. This number does not represent the full picture. You will be using it to work out your debt ratio, which is the amount of debt you owe relative to the amount of money you earn. This is something that banks also work out when you are applying for a mortgage.

The banks will usually work it out in terms of monthly payments, but it is easier to use our gross income for us. Divide the total amount of debt you owe by your yearly gross income. The number you see is your debt ratio. So if you have $25,000 of debt and an annual salary of $50,000, your debt ratio will be 0.5. If you have $150,000 of debt and your salary remains $50,000, your debt ratio is 2.5. The bigger the margin between your income and your debt, the larger your debt ratio.

Paying off debt is much easier if the ratio is under 1. This means that you earn more than what you have to pay off. By cutting back, saving where you can, and increasing your monthly repayments, you will be able to pay this debt off quite quickly, perhaps even in a year if you are really serious.

When your debt ratio is above 1, you have a little more work to do. Your goal is to first get that ratio under 1 because you will never be able to cut back enough to pay off your whole debt in a short space of time while receiving the same salary. Keep making payments and pay off as much as you can until you can lower your debt ratio. It is definitely possible to pay off debt, even a considerable amount of debt. As long as you are committed and are willing to make the necessary sacrifices, you can do it!

Keep checking and working out your ratio as you pay off your debt. Sometimes it is difficult to feel like you are making progress when you still see large amounts of debt. The debt ratio is a more manageable number to keep track of. As you see the number decreasing, you will be more motivated to keep going. Remember that both a decrease in the amount of debt and a salary increase will bring down your debt ratio.

Change the Behaviors That Got You Into Debt

There are many different reasons why people get into debt.

Some take out student loans to complete their degrees. Others suffer from job loss or even expensive medical bills. Then there is the top reason that people get into debt, which is living outside of their means. People have a nasty habit of trying to keep up with the Joneses. That becomes a major problem when the Joneses earn a household salary of $100,000 and you only $50,000.

Regardless of why you got into debt, the important thing is that you never do it again. Putting up guardrails in your life will help protect you from falling into the same trap again or making your current debt situation worse. If you got into debt due to student loans, do not take out an extra loan for another master's degree or even a Ph.D. It may sound like a good idea and a noble pursuit, but if you can't afford it, you should look into other avenues of funding your studies or wait until you actually can afford it.

If you got into debt by losing employment or having to pay for unexpected medical bills, make sure you have a savings account with some emergency funds. Unfortunately, in life, unexpected things happen. These things cannot be planned for, but we can still make sure that we are prepared for them. Having an emergency fund ready is crucial to making sure you stay out of debt.

For those currently in debt, your priority is getting out of it and then set up your emergency fund. If you are overrun with debt because of lavish spending when you did not have the means to do so, then some habits need to be broken.

You have to know how much money you can spend and then stick to it. As soon as you start using credit to buy things that are not necessities, it is a slippery slope into debt. There are really only a few necessities: Food, housing, utilities, and transport. Everything else can be done without, so if you find yourself swiping for a new pair of Nike sneakers, you will need to reshuffle your priorities.

Even within those necessities, people can easily go overboard. Food is essential, but eating out at fancy restaurants is not. Housing is important, but living in a four-bedroom house when you can only afford a two-bedroom apartment is going to get you in trouble. You need to have transport, but you do not need the new Mercedes Benz. If you really want to improve your debt situation, you will have to be honest about how much you can afford and then stick to that budget.

Earn Enough to Get Out Of Debt

In order to get out of debt, you need to be earning more than you are spending. The larger the margin is between the amount you have to spend on necessities and the amount you are earning every month, the quicker you will be able to pay off your debt. Cutting back and spending less are great strategies for getting out of debt, but there is only so far it can take you if you have a lot of debt.

Increasing the amount you earn will allow you to pay off your debt quicker. It may not be what most people like to hear, but it is the truth. To do this, you may have to think about switching your career, starting a business, or getting a second job. If you make the right moves, you will increase your salary significantly. There is always an opportunity if you are looking out for it.

There are also other things you could do to increase your income. Selling unnecessary items that you own could give you a nice boost to help pay off debt. Eventually, you will run out of stuff to sell, so this isn't a long-term solution but can help collect a large initial amount to pay into your debt balance. If your job pays overtime, you could put in extra hours to get some extra cash.

Lastly, you can ask for a raise or work toward a promotion. Many people do not get raises or promotions because they do not ask. Companies often want to save money where they can, so if you are willing to work for less, they will be happy with that. If you are going to ask for a raise or promotion, just make sure you have worked hard enough to deserve it. You will probably have to state your case for the pay increase, so you have to have a good argument.

<u>Make More Than the Minimum Payment</u>

If you want to get out of debt, you will have to pay more than the bare minimum on your debt. The longer you have the debt, the more internet it will rack up, which means the more you will have to pay in the long run. This means that paying off your debt helps you twofold. It lessens your debt, and it lessens the interest it will incur.

You already know how much the minimum amount payable is. All you have to do is pay an extra every month. Just make sure that the loan you are paying off does not charge any prepayment penalties. These penalties are charged if you pay the loan off before the loan term ends. This would have been stipulated when you took out the loan.

Negotiate Bills and Lower Interest

If you feel overwhelmed by the interest you are incurring on your debt, it might be a good idea to ask for a lower interest rate. This is actually pretty common with credit card issuers. They will often lower the interest if you have a good record with them. If you have been up to date with all your payments and you make payments on time, you have a good shot at a lower interest rate.

It's not just credit cards that can be negotiated down in this way. Medical bills, car repayments, internet services, and rent payments are all negotiation options. All it takes is for you to get on the phone. Medical bills can be negotiated down if you offer to pay them off immediately at a discounted rate. Depending on the car dealership, you may also be able to do the same with car payments.

Also, look into negotiating your car insurance rates. Car insurance companies and internet service providers are in a highly competitive market. This means that they will be willing to negotiate if you say that you can get a better deal somewhere else. Do some research and see the market prices before you get on the phone with them.

Basically, any kind of bill can be negotiated under the right circumstance. If you think you are overpaying on something, don't be afraid to approach another service provider and ask for a lower rate. Any money saved can help you get closer to your goal of being debt-free. If you think about it, there is nothing to lose if you just ask. The worst-case scenario is that they say no, and you have to carry on as normal. However, the savings you will receive if they say yes could be massive, and that is worth it.

Use Found Money to Pay Debt Faster

Found money is money you will come across at some point that is not part of your regular income. This can be from a yearly increase, bonuses, tax refunds, an inheritance, or even money you receive as a gift. You will probably come across some sort of found money during the year. Instead of buying something unnecessary, use it to pay off your debt.

If you take that money and put it toward your debt repayment, you will have taken a nice chunk out of what you owe. Found money is never calculated into a budget, so you really won't miss it if you never get to spend it. It will be better to pay off debt than to buy something nice.

Do a Balance Transfer

A balance transfer is essentially paying off one credit card with another. It works when you have a card with a high-interest rate and transfer the debt to one with a lower interest rate. Some cards will offer you a 0% APR for a specific amount of time. This allows you to save on the interest you would have been paying on the old card. If you can, try to pay off the debt before the 0% APR period ends.

You may have to pay a balance transfer fee when you do this. If the fee is higher than what you would be saving in interest, then you should not do it. The fee will depend on which card issuer you sign up with. There are a few that offer no fees, so do your research and see what you can find. If you have good credit and are making payments on time, you will have a better chance of getting a good balance transfer deal.

Use a Personal Loan to Consolidate the Credit Card Debt

Paying off debt outright will always be the best option, but if you are struggling with credit card debt, taking out a personal loan might be a solution for you. This is especially helpful if you have lots of debt on different cards and accounts or the interest is way too high. However, you have to make sure that the loan you take out is of lower interest than what you are paying right now. Otherwise, you might end up paying more.

It will be in your best interest to thoroughly research different loan providers and find one that offers the best deal. Take into account both the rates and fees you might have to pay. Once you have selected your loan, you can go through the process and pay off your other debt. Immediately start paying off the loan according to the terms agreed upon. Try to pay off this loan as quickly as possible.

<u>Do Not Take on More Debt</u>

It is probably the most important thing you need to remember. When you are trying to pay off your debt, do not take on more of it! Racking up debt can be a habit, which will get you in trouble. Do not fall for anything that might get you into more debt. While you are paying off your accounts, you need to be laser-focused. You really do not need anything new at this point. You are saying no now, but only so that you can have the freedom to say yes to whatever you want in the future.

If you can keep focused on just paying off your debt, you will be so thankful to yourself. There is nothing like the feeling of being debt-free. You are not bound by anything, and you do not owe anyone any more of your money. As soon as all of your debt is paid off, your money is yours and you can do whatever you want with it.

Try One of These Methods to Getting Out Debt

People use many methods to pay off debt, but the following two are by far the most popular. They are the avalanche method and the snowball method. They both aim to help you pay off your debt as soon as possible, but they go about it in almost opposite ways.

You will have to pick the one that will work best for you. There have been many success stories that have come out of both methods.

The important thing is that you evaluate your habits and thought patterns to make sure you pick the one that will keep you motivated to pay off your debt as fast as possible. You can use all of the above tips in conjunction with either of these two methods to help pay off your debt as fast as possible.

Avalanche Method

This method starts you off with paying the debt with the highest interest first and then moving down the list until all the debt is paid. Naturally, the first thing you will need to do is list out your debt, starting from the one with the highest interest. The amount you need to pay back is not significant right now. Once you have the list, you will know where you are starting and which debt gets the attention after the prior one is paid off.

You should note that you will still pay the minimum on all your debt and just be more aggressive with the higher-interest one. Please don't stop paying off the other debts altogether. Any extra cash that you have will go immediately into the high-interest debt. Every time you pay off an account, you will free up money to pay the other accounts. As you get lower and lower on the list, you will start paying it off faster and faster. That's why it is called the avalanche method.

It's like snow racing down the mountain, gaining more momentum the further it gets.

Since you will be paying off the highest interest first, you will be saving more money in the long run. The highest-interest rate debt is usually the toughest to get rid of because of the rate it accrues the interest. The only downside here is that it will take a while to see any progress. You will have to keep going even when you don't feel like you are making progress. As soon as you can knock the first account off the list, it will get much easier, and the process will speed up. You just have to stick with it and be patient at the beginning.

Snowball Method

This method is a better fit for those that need small wins to gain momentum and keep them motivated. You start off with the smallest amount of debt first and then work your way up to the highest. You will not be taking into account the interest rate. If you have lots of accounts with smaller amounts of debt, this method will be perfect for you. Once you have paid off the smallest debt, you will use the money you now have free to put toward the next smallest debt, and so on.

Like with the avalanche method, you will still be paying the minimum on all the other debt you have, just focusing any extra money on one debt at a time. As you keep paying off these smaller debts, you will gain momentum and keep freeing up more and more money to put into the next debt, essentially like how a snowball starts off small and gains momentum by getting larger and larger. Reducing the number of debt accounts you have will also be better for your credit score, so it is good to keep that in mind.

The downside to this method is that it does not take the interest rate into account. It means that you might pay more in the long run because the higher-interest accounts will still be gaining that interest. The longer you leave the high-interest accounts, the more you will be paying over time. It might be a worthwhile trade-off if you need motivation and momentum quickly. Essentially you are trying to pay off the debt in the best way you can.

Many people really struggle to pay off debt because it feels like a never-ending battle. The small wins allow you to feel like you are going somewhere. It is easier to keep going and feel motivated if there is proof that what you are doing is working. If you have tried to get out of debt in the past and have never been able to stick to it, this might be the method for you.

Chapter 4

SAVE YOUR MONEY

As you have probably gathered by this point, the biggest determinant of whether you will reach financial independence is how well you can save. Your savings will be the backbone of your retirement. Not only is it crucial to save for your retirement, but you need to be able to save where you can once you are retired. The habits and principles you set in place now will help carry you through your entire retirement.

Keep Track of Everything You Spend

Keep a notebook on you or have a note-taking app downloaded on your phone at all times. Every time you buy something, write it down. Every single dollar should be accounted for, even if you spent a few cents on a piece of chewing gum.

At the end of the day, review where your money went and see if you could have saved or done without something you bought. Doing this will help you control your expenses. You will get a good idea of what you spend versus what you actually need to live. It will be easier to stop spending your money on certain things when you can see that it is not needed. Once you are fully aware of what you spend, you will have a clearer perspective on your finances.

We often do not realize how much the little purchases add up in the end. A candy bar here and a cup of coffee there might end up with you spending hundreds of dollars a month unnecessarily. Sure, you can track it on your banking app, but there is something different about writing it down. It is almost like an accountability partner. Eventually, when you see how everything adds up, you will be less likely to buy these smaller items and will save quite a lot of money in the process.

Review Your Biggest Expenses

The first step in saving money and planning your finances is to review your most significant expenses. These are your car and housing payments, which are the biggest chunks of your salary. Trying to save money on the smaller things is wise, but you first have to manage the main ones. You might be losing out on hundreds of dollars because you are not handling these expenses in the right way. Let's break it down and see where you can be saving money on these big expenses.

Car

The first thing you need to ask yourself is, do you even need a car in the first place? Cars are money siphons, they just suck it all up, and if people were honest with themselves, many would not even need to own one. Owning a car is seen as a milestone that everyone has to reach.

Do you remember the show *My Super Sweet Sixteen*? They would throw an extravagant party for their 16th birthday, and every single one of them would get a car. Subconsciously we all think that owning a car signifies freedom and adulthood. Many people also use cars to show off their wealth; the better the car, the more wealthy they are. Every single thing in this paragraph is not a mindset that we should adopt.

Cars are, in fact, not a milestone. They do not signify freedom, and having a fancy one does not mean you are rich. The saying that cars are an investment is simply not true. If you buy a brand-new car, it loses about half its value when you drive it off the lot. If you ask me, that is not a very good investment. Not to mention the services you have to pay for every year, insurance, gas, and forking out money every time something goes wrong with it.

When you think about it, it all adds up. When you review your car expenses, take all of this into account.

Weigh up how much you spend in a year on your car and see if you would be able to spend less if you were to use public transport or a car service like Uber. If you live in a big city, it is usually better to take public transport so that you can skip traffic, which is certainly a bonus.

Take a look at your car repayments and see if there is a way to save. Sometimes selling your car and purchasing a cheaper secondhand car is the better option. Buying a secondhand car is much smarter than buying a brand-new one off the lot. If you get a secondhand car inspected before you buy it and it has low mileage, it will last you just as long as any brand-new car, and you will get it for a fraction of the price.

Also, look for a car that is smaller and more fuel-efficient. If you do need a car, going for the cheapest option is the best thing to do. Cheap does not mean that it is not good quality.

Housing Payments or Rent

Housing or rent will probably be your biggest expense. If it is not, I highly recommend going over your financial statements because you are overpaying somewhere. Owning a large house in an affluent suburb seems to be everyone's goal. Just like with the car, it is all keeping up with the Joneses. You end up spending unnecessary money on a house that is too big for you.

When it comes to houses, it is not just the monthly payments you have to worry about but also the upkeep, general maintenance, and any other expenses that might pop up. If you already own a house and have paid it off, that's great. You have significantly less to worry about than other people who are still paying off their houses. You should still take a look at what you are paying for things related to the house, like insurance and property tax. Perhaps moving to another suburb or downsizing could reduce these costs significantly.

If you are currently paying off a house or thinking of buying one, you should be looking for realistic ways to cut down on what you are paying. Of course, the bigger the house, the more you will be paying. The more affluent the suburb, the more it will cost you to live there. Try to go for the smallest space you would be happy living in. Picking the largest house is one of the quickest ways to waste your money and get into debt. Always shop around before making a decision.

There are bound to be houses that are just what you are looking for but in a different suburb or area. When getting a loan for your house, you should also shop around. You should never just settle on the first offer you get because there might be something better around the corner. Informed decisions will save you a ton of money. Remember that this is a competitive market, and you could get a better deal by just saying that you found something better through another company.

Renting might be the better option for you, so don't rule it out just yet. In many cases, renting is cheaper than buying a house. If you plan to move around after you retire or travel for long periods, renting would make more sense. There is no point paying for a house you will hardly be using. Renting also makes you more flexible so that you can move around. If your goal is to change cities when you leave your job, buying a house could hold you back.

At the end of the day, it is your choice to rent or buy a home. Everyone's situation is different and therefore needs a different solution. Take into account your lifestyle and your goals. Both of these will help you decide on what is better for you.

Small But Useful Saving Tips

The smaller things that you do could lead to huge savings in the long run. Smaller amounts that go out of your account without paying much attention can actually lead to you spending way more than what you think. Learning how to control your smaller impulses will be better for you and your bank account.

<u>Choose Your Bank Accounts Wisely</u>

Not all bank accounts were created equal. Some have great perks and benefits that can help you save a bit of extra money. Do some research and make sure that your bank gives you the best deal and benefits possible. Some banks offer rewards for certain activities, so do some research and see if you can make small changes to earn some of these bonuses.

They can vary from cashback to free meals at certain restaurants. You will also find that some will offer more attractive interest rates. Look for the bank that will benefit you the most, and make sure you are not overpaying for your account.

Set Up an Automatic Saving

Saving is essentially paying yourself. When your savings automatically leaves your account, you are paying yourself first. Having the money leave your account as soon as you receive your salary every month is the best way to ensure that you are putting money away. When we are given a choice between spending our money now and saving it for later, we now often win because we want to satisfy our instant gratification.

An automatic saving removes any temptation because the money is out of your account before it has reached your hands. You can set this amount to whatever you want and then add extra savings as you go through the month. The important thing is that the bulk of your savings will already be tucked away, and anything extra is a bonus.

Ditch Watching TV

If you are an avid TV watcher, you might want to know that it might be the reason that you are spending so much money. That is not only due to cable's price but also because of the advertisements you watch in your favorite shows. Advertising agencies work hard to make their ads look very attractive and make you want to buy their products. Whether you know it or not, you are affected by it.

At the moment, you are watching the ad and not really thinking about it, but once you pass the item in the shop or while you are browsing an online store, your brain switches. You remember seeing that thing somewhere, so it must be worth it to give it a try. Ads influence our spending habits more than we think.

There are other benefits to not having a TV. You will have a lower electric bill, plus you get to funnel that time into something more productive, like a side hustle. If you can't give up on having something to watch, pay for a streaming service subscription like Netflix or Amazon Prime Video. They are relatively cheap and there are no ads. All the money you save can be directly funneled into your savings.

<u>Commit to the 30 Day Rule</u>

We can all fall into the trap of buying stuff unnecessarily because we love instant gratification. We see something and want it now, so before we have time to think about it, we have added it to the cart and are on the way to checkout. I think we would all be truly surprised at the amount of money we have wasted on things that we bought on a whim.

To prevent this from happening, commit to keeping the "30-day rule". It states that if you want something, you cannot purchase it for 30 days. If you still want it after the month is over, you can go ahead and buy it. You will see that you will not want most of the things you thought you did after the time has passed. This time allows you to think about it and get over the initial feeling of wanting it.

There are very few things that you absolutely need right now, so you won't be depriving yourself of anything by following this rule. You will feel much more satisfied after waiting if you do need the item and are now able to buy it. It is a win on all fronts.

Do Saving Challenges

Often there are these saving challenges that circulate at the start of every new year. It comes from the "new year, new me" mentality. Although you won't be doing these challenges as a resolution, they can still help you save a bit of extra cash, and we know that every little bit helps you reach your goal quicker.

One of these challenges is the 100 envelope challenge. All you have to do is get 100 envelopes and label them from 1 to 100. Each day, place the same amount of money in the envelope as is written on the envelope. I know this may sound silly, but by the time you are done, you would have saved $5,050. That adds up and you will probably not even feel it until it gets to the later stages. You could also double or triple the amount of money you put in the envelope if you want more of a challenge and save more money.

There are plenty of saving challenges that circulate on social media platforms. If you come across one, use it as an opportunity to give your savings account an extra boost.

Do Not Go Shopping Without a List

This tip applies to all kinds of shopping. The typical list to make is the grocery list, but you should have a list for every area. It includes the drug store, clothing stores, and even hardware stores. The truth is that if you walk into a store without a plan, you will think you need every single nice thing that you see, and you will be able to justify it to yourself. Do not fall into that trap.

If you have a list, you have to stick to it. There is no point in adding stuff to the list when you get to the store. If you didn't plan for it in advance, it does not get to go into the basket. If you do not shop with a grocery list already, it is time you make one. The grocery store is where most people waste their money. Food always looks nice, and you will want to try the new flavor of Doritos when you see it. Creating a list is like putting on blinders and making sure you stay focused on the right things. It will also help you reduce food waste, which is another bonus.

Having a list also stops you from being swayed by sales. If you did not need it when it was full price, you do not need it now that it has a red SALE sticker on it. You are really not saving $20 if you buy something for $15 that used to be $35. You have just wasted $15 on something you would never have bought had it been under normal circumstances.

Get Into Meal Planning

Meal planning is one of the easiest ways to save money.

If you know what you will be eating for the week, you will know what you have to buy. So this tip is a precursor to the last one. You must know what you need to create an accurate grocery shopping list.

You are more likely to stick within your budget if you know what you will be eating for the week. It lessens the chance of you buying unnecessary food just in case. You will also be able to plan to make cheaper meals. There are plenty of cheap meals that can be made that will save you money.Meal planning also reduces food waste, which is good for your wallet and the planet.

If you know you are making a dish that needs fresh vegetables, you can buy them on that day rather than just buy a bunch of products and hope you will use them. Just try meal planning for a week and see how much money you save by not buying unnecessary food items at the store.

Do Not Be a Brand Loyalist

Nowadays, it is so easy to fall into loyalty to one brand. Maybe you have used it for as long as you remember, or you have some sort of connection to them. It can actually be costing you. Staying fixated on one brand means that you will not be aware of a better deal somewhere else.

When it comes to food items and even clothes, the brand does not matter. You can pick up something for almost the exact same quality but at half the price if you are willing to switch brands. Fancier brands often spend more effort and money on marketing and making their product seem better when there are only slight differences between them.

<u>Skip the Coffee Run</u>

So much money is wasted on coffee every single day. Going to your favorite coffee shop for your morning fix costs you more than you think. In fact, one-third of Americans are spending more money on coffee than on investing. That means that they are spending more money on a caffeine fix than investing in their future and making more money. When you look at it like that, it sounds crazy.

I'm not saying that coffee is wrong, but there are cheaper ways to get it. You can make coffee at home with instant coffee, or you can buy a coffee maker. Both of these options are cheaper, and honestly, I've tasted better coffee made at home than ones from coffee stores. If you really love your Starbucks, they sell Starbucks instant coffee at grocery stores, which is significantly cheaper than at the coffee shop itself.

If you are thinking about the convenience of just quickly popping out to get a coffee, I can guarantee you that making the coffee at home is much more convenient. You can switch on the kettle or coffee machine and let it run while doing something else. Your coffee will be ready in a few minutes, and you didn't even need to get dressed. It also saves you money on gas for driving to the coffee shop and prevents you from the temptation of buying an unnecessary confectionery item as well.

<u>Quit Smoking</u>

I know this is a bit of a touchy subject for some. It is not meant to knock anyone's lifestyle choices, but smoking does cost a lot of money. Depending on what brand you smoke and how often, the amount you will pay for a smoking habit varies. But let's just work on an average amount of $6.65 per pack. If you smoke two to three packs a week, that costs you between $693.60 to $1037.40 a year. Over ten years that amounts to more than $10,000 extra that could have been collecting interest in your savings account.

If you are a smoker, you have often heard these types of things. Just take some time to carefully consider the pros and cons. Kicking the habit could end up saving you thousands of dollars in the long run.

<u>Buy a Reusable Water Bottle</u>

The bottled water industry made about $2.5 billion in 2016, and it is probably more now. That is a lot of money for something that comes out of our taps at home. Buying a reusable water bottle will stop you from having to buy water wherever you go out somewhere. You may not think it is a big deal, but it can add up. Either way, it is not very smart to pay for something you can technically get for free or for a minuscule fraction of the cost.

I know the argument here is that you don't like the taste of tap water. Then why not install a filter? You would still be saving more money than if you were to keep buying bottled water. It's definitely worth a try, and there is nothing wrong with tap water. The added "vitamins and minerals" are not providing your body with many benefits in any case because they are in such a small amount.

Eat at Home

Americans waste so much money on eating out or ordering in. The price you would pay to make the food yourself is a fraction of what a restaurant or fast food place would charge you. Many people are put off because cooking at home takes time and energy. That is true if you were to make very elaborate meals every day, but most midweek meals take about 30 minutes to prepare, which, if you think about it, is quicker than ordering and waiting for your food to be delivered to you.

Invest in a good cookbook or watch a YouTube video on meal ideas. There are plenty of quick and delicious recipes out there. You can make cooking efficient if you plan your meals for the week in advance. For example, you could roast a whole chicken on Monday and have it with roast potatoes. The leftovers can be shredded and used to make salads, sandwiches, and tacos for lunch and dinner for however long they will last. That means you are really only cooking on Monday, and for the next day or so, you are just using what you already have.

This sort of planning makes cooking at home cheaper and more efficient than ordering food elsewhere. This tip also flows over into lunch at work. You should always pack a lunch rather than buying something when you get there. We tend to overspend and overestimate how much we can eat when we are hungry, and because of this, we end up buying way too much food. This is costly. Instead, if you already have food there, you will just eat what you have brought. There is no risk of buying food unnecessarily, and it is much healthier for both you and your bank balance.

Reduce Energy Cost

Cutting down on your home's energy use saves you money and reduces the pollution generated by non-renewable sources of energy. Do you know that you can save money on your electric bill just by making a few simple tweaks to your home? Don't worry. These small, everyday changes in your power consumption are easy to make.

Start with some simple things like checking seals on windows and doors, taking shorter showers and replacing your showerhead, fixing leaky ductworks, washing your clothes in cold tap water, and installing LED lightbulbs and dimmer switches.

While energy-efficient appliances (fridge, washing machine, etc.) are a great way to save money on your electric bill, they are quite expensive! But if you add their cost to your monthly budget, you can save money right away, and those improvements will pay for themselves over time.

Use Cash Instead of Card

We live in a digital world, which means it is much easier to use your card than carry around cash. The card's problem is that all your funds are in there, and it isn't easy to keep track of how much you are spending. If you have the cash, you know exactly how much you have to spend that day. Once it is gone, it is gone, and there is nothing much you can do about it. It is a great way to take control of your spending.

A great way to do this is to draw out all the cash you have for spending money for the month, then divide it into weekly amounts. Every week, you can place the allotted amount in your wallet and spend that however you want. If you spend it all on Monday, you do not get to buy anything for the rest of the week.

If you do not spend all of the money by the end of the week, the extra will be put forward to the next week.

Alternatively, any extra can be added to your savings because it is likely that you have budgeted for each week and don't need that extra money.

It may seem like it is tiresome to keep drawing out the cash, but you will definitely benefit from this if you're someone who struggles with spending. In general, we spend less when we have to spend cash because the actual trading of money for goods is more real to us than just swiping our cards. We can ignore the bank notifications when the money comes out of our account, but we cannot ignore the physical cash leaving our hands when we buy something.

Remove Your Credit Card From Online Shopping Accounts

Online shopping is so easy to do. You can easily find yourself on a website when you are bored or have some time to kill. If your credit card details are already saved on the site, it just takes a few clicks, and you have purchased something that you probably do not need. Make sure that you do not make it so easy for yourself. Never save your credit card details on a site.

Whenever you want to buy something, you will have to manually dig out your card and enter all the details. It creates some resistance before the purchase and gives you some time to think about whether you need the item or not. It will also force you to think about if the item is worth the added effort of finding the card and entering all the details. Often we realize it is not worth it and then don't end up buying the item.

Chapter 5

GENERATE PASSIVE INCOME

When someone mentions passive income, it gets a somewhat missed reception. Some people are angry or defensive because they find it hard to believe that there is a better way to make money than what they have been doing at their traditional nine to five.

Some get excited because they think passive income is getting money for nothing. Others are confused about how you are even able to build passive income. I think all of these reactions stem from a place of not fully understanding what passive income is. Passive income is not just receiving free money. In most cases, it takes hard work, at least initially.

When you aim to create a passive income, you are doing something that will still bring in money long after you have put in the work. You put in the work now and then reap the benefits later. It is not some big money-making hack; it is just a different way to make money that gives you a better return on investment of your time.

You have to understand that you may not see results immediately with many forms of passive income. It may take a while before you can bring in enough cash to support yourself. If you are willing to take the leap, you will thank yourself later. Pursuing any form of passive income will help you reach your financial freedom goal much quicker.

Just to clarify, passive income is not a get-rich-quick scheme. It will definitely not make you rich overnight. Depending on what you decide to do to build passive income, it may never be enough to support you on its own or might take many years before it builds up to that point. The goal is to be able to make enough money to give yourself a little more freedom financially. You could add this additional income to your savings for FIRE, or if you have already reached FIRE, then you have extra money to increase your standard of living should you wish.

Another thing to keep in mind is that passive income works best when you have multiple income streams. This way, even if you are only getting a few hundred dollars from each one, together they can make you a decent salary. The best thing you can do is choose a few things that sound interesting to you and try them out. Chances are that not everyone will be a resounding success, but you will come out with a few that will stick. These are the ones that will continue making you money for years to come.

If you feel you do not have time right now to try some of these out, that's ok. When you have reached financial freedom, it could be the perfect time to pick one of these up. Many of these things are fun and can be creative outlets, so when you have the time to dive in, you can go for it. Trying to get an additional income source will never go to waste, even if you have already reached your FIRE goal.

Now that you know what passive income is and what it entails, let's work on some ideas to help you bring in the money. There are always more ways to make some money on the side, so if you find a way to make passive income that is not listed, you should still go for it!

Make Money With a Blog

Starting a blog is a great way to make money if you have some information to share. There are thousands of topics and niches to build your blog from. The biggest struggle will be narrowing it down so that the content is relevant and specific enough that it is helpful to readers. People will read blog posts that give them information that they have not found anywhere else.

If you are under the impression that starting a blog will be easy, you should think again. Consistency and valuable information will be key to a successful blog. You want to have something that attracts people to the information you are offering. You also need to be putting out enough blog posts that you have a higher chance of reaching people and becoming well known.

The more traffic your blog can generate, the more profitable it will be. Look for niches that are not overrun with competition. The less competition, the better because people will automatically be directed to your page. Well-researched, well-written blog posts can generate income for years without much upkeep.

There are plenty of search results that are a few years old on the first page of Google. They manage to keep their position because their information was relevant, and they have kept it updated. Updating information does not take that much effort, but it does mean that you have to be in the loop of your writing niche. That is why it is better to write about something you know and are interested in.

The goal is to get as popular as you can and gain exposure. There are plenty of ways to do this, including promoting yourself on social media, using paid advertisements, and cross-promoting on other pages. Cross-promoting is a perfect way to get followers interested in your content. You could partner with other blogs and websites that work in similar niches. If you strike a deal where you both cross-promote each other, you will not have to pay anything for the extra money for getting your name out there.

You probably know that you can't make money by just writing the blog. What generates revenue is people paying for advertising space and affiliate marketing. Let's dive a little more into those aspects.

Affiliate Marketing

Affiliate marketing is when you post a link to a product on another website or online shop and get paid every time someone uses your link to purchase something. You will get a portion of the sales made. It's basically like a commission for sales.

There are plenty of brands or products you can work with to market their items. It is always best to find something related to your niche. If you have a blog about car mechanics, posting an affiliate link to a sewing kit will not make you any money. It is all about providing value to your readers. The more the reader feels like they need what you are linking to, the higher the chance they will buy it.

Advertising

Having a blog means that you own online real estate. This real estate can be used to advertise other people's products. Brands and companies are always looking for advertising space. If you provide that space, you can earn a passive income for it.

These companies hire ad networks who are the middleman between you and the companies. You are basically being paid to do nothing. Depending on the traffic your blog gets, you could easily make a large sum of money, even when you are sleeping.

Buy a Blog

If you are interested in having a blog but do not want to go through all the effort to start one up and build it from scratch, you can buy an existing blog. The internet is in no shortage of blogs, and there are plenty of people who want to sell their blogs because they simply do not have the time or will to keep up with it. If the blog already has a decent amount of traffic, you will be buying a proper source of passive income. Everything has been established, and the affiliates and advertisements are already set up. Everything will just be transferred straight to you.

Often these blogs sell for about 24 times the amount they make per month, so it might take a bit of initial cash for you to invest in it. However, you will be able to turn over a profit in two years, which is not that long if you think about it, especially since you will not have to do anything for it.

If you want to see a profit sooner, you could add some fresh content to generate more traffic. Building onto the blog will allow you to make back your money quicker and ultimately see more profit from the blog. If you research, you will be able to buy a blog with evergreen content, which means that it will bring in money long after it has gone silent.

Diversify

Once you have gained popularity on one platform, you can carry that following over to other platforms. You could set up a YouTube channel or an Instagram page where you post related content but slightly different from your blog.

You will not only attract a new following but be able to carry your current following throughout the different platforms. You will be making money in the same way as the blog, through advertising and affiliate marketing. With Instagram and YouTube, you could also get sponsored by brands to promote certain products. It will add another way to bring in some money.

The more platforms you have, the more opportunities you get to make money. You will still have to produce relevant and entertaining content. If you do end up getting big enough, you could get someone to run certain pages for you. It will mean that these platforms become purely passive income.

Rent Out a Room

If you have a spare room, cottage, apartment, or any other kind of living space, you can rent that out for cash. It requires minimal effort on your part, and you can make a reasonable sum of money for it. Depending on the space you have, you could rent it out permanently or do something like an AirBnB where you rent it out to people on holiday.

Renting your space out to holidaymakers through AirBnB or privately can be more lucrative than a permanent residence set-up. It is dependent on how busy you are. If you want your place to be successful, you will have to put in effort to make it look nice. The most successful AirBnBs are the ones that are Instagram-worthy. Take some time to research design trends and make the space feel homey and welcoming.

Positive experiences will get reviewed and increase the traffic to your space. I would be lying if I were to say that this is a pure source of passive income. You will have to go in between visitors and do a clean-up and restock to ensure that everything is up to scratch. Honestly, this is not that much work. It will probably take a few minutes to an hour, depending on the place's size and if the guests were tidy or not. People tend to respect an AirBnB more because it is someone's home, so it is implausible that you will have someone that completely turns the space upside down.

Create Digital Products

Living in a world run by technology and the internet has opened the doors to many different ways to bring in some extra cash. Digital products are something that everyone uses in some form, so if you can create something that people find useful, you can make a ton of money from it.

Digital products are a great source of income because they are low investment and potentially high yield. There are virtually no start-up fees, and distribution and delivery are not factors. Once you produce your digital product and put it online, people are free to buy and download it whenever they feel like it. Here are some great digital product ideas that you can try out.

Stock Photos

If you have a DSLR camera or even just a smartphone with a great camera, you can take photos that people will want to buy. Stock photos often get a bad reputation because we automatically think of a random model posing awkwardly with a white background. These do exist, but now you can get stunning stock photos that can be used for all sorts of things.

Take a look at the website Shutterstock (or Adobe Stock) if you need proof or inspiration. You don't have to be a professional photographer to sell stock photos. Some of the photos are taken of random things. Empty rooms, road traffic signs, crowds of people, and many other everyday sightings. All you have to do is have your camera handy to take a few snaps. The photos do have to be good quality and nice to look at. If you have an eye for photography, this could be a great fit.

There are plenty of places where you could sell your photos online. All it will take is a little research to find them. Look into platforms like Shutterstock and iStockPhoto. These platforms may charge a fee for every photo you sell.

The best way to make a fair amount of money through photos is to have a large portfolio. The more photos you have up, the higher your chances of getting them sold. One photo can be bought multiple times, which provides a continuous stream of income. Also, try to upload your photos onto more than one website. The more your photos are seen, the greater the chance of selling them.

Similar to stock photos are stock videos, especially those filmed with a drone. It can be quite lucrative because not many people have drones, so this market is less competitive. People need these kinds of videos for various productions and projects. You will need a drone and a license for this, but you can always rent one to take some really cool videos if you do not own one.

The most in-demand footage at the moment is nature footage of coastlines, forests, and mountains; urban footage of cities, skylines, roads, and architecture; picturesque travel locations; sports events; and large crowds of people, whether it be in busy streets, festivals, or events.

Apps

Everyone has a smartphone or tablet, and one thing that we all do is download apps. These can be meal-tracking apps, games, daily planners, exercise apps, you name it. Building a useful app will allow you to have a continuous stream of passive income.

Many people just download apps for fun to see what they are. If your app is interesting enough, you could get a good amount of followers. If you go onto the app store, you will see that some apps are free and others you need to pay for. It's not just the apps that need to be bought that make money. Free apps make money through selling advertising space, just like a blog. You will see when you download most free apps, you will need to watch a video to do a specific action, there are banner ads somewhere on the screen, or at random times ads will just pop up.

Of course, to build an app, you will need to learn how to code. There are plenty of coding classes on the web; take one if you do not already know how to code. Who knows, you could find that you are good at it. The other option is to hire a developer to build your app for you. It can be an expensive initial investment, but if your idea is excellent and unique, it could be worth it.

You could also look into hiring a student developer, someone who has not yet finished their studies. Hiring one of them will be significantly cheaper, and you could still get a really great app out of it. Offering the experience and something to add to their resume is always attractive to a student.

If you are planning on building an app, try to make it as unique as possible. There are thousands of apps out there, and the competition can be stiff. Choosing a niche that does not have many competitors might be your best bet. If you try breaking into a quite competitive market, make sure that your app offers something different. That will give you an edge and make you stand out from the rest.

Templates

Templates are extremely helpful to people who want to get something done but do not have the time to sit and start from scratch. Templates can be for wedding invitations, guest lists, party planning, Excel spreadsheets, or resumes. It is much easier to fill in the required information than design something yourself.

Some other ideas for useful templates are business planning templates, contracts, WordPress themes, and business card templates. You can probably make a template for just about anything that will make people's lives easier. The more you create and put out, the higher the chance of making a good amount of money.

Craft Patterns

The craft and the DIY market is undoubtedly growing. People love making things by themselves but sometimes need a little help. These patterns are the same things as templates. You will be creating something that other people can follow to make something. Sewing, knitting, paper crafts, and painting patterns are all things that are in demand.

You can sell your patterns on Etsy, which has a considerable following in the craft and DIY market. You could also look into selling printables. These are coloring pages, workbooks, and things like DIY birthday cards. People will download it and make it their own based on the design you have created.

Write an eBook

If you have some information you want to share or a story idea you would like to create, why not look into writing an ebook? Self-publishing is great if you have ever had the desire to write a book because it allows you to skip the hassle of getting a publisher on board, and it is much cheaper in the long run. Even today, in a world that is overrun with various forms of entertainment and information, books still come out on top.

All you need is an idea and a computer to get started. There are plenty of niches and genres to choose from. Take a look on Amazon if you are looking for ideas. You will probably be quite overwhelmed with the number of topics to write about. You do not have to stop at one book. The more you have, the better because there is a high chance that the following you create for one book can be carried over to your other books. People who like a specific author tend to buy many of their books.

If you have a brilliant idea for an ebook but do not have the time to write it or perhaps aren't confident in your writing skill, you could always hire someone to write it for you. It requires an initial investment, but it can pay off once your book takes off. Getting it designed, edited, and marketed is also something you could look into to give your book a boost. The length of your book can vary. Some are quite short while others are very long. As long as you provide quality information, the length is not too much of a concern.

You can sell your ebook on many different platforms, like Amazon or Lulu. You could also sell the book through your website or use it as a lead magnet if you have another digital product that you are selling. Ebooks that are used as lead magnets are usually shorter than regular books. However you decide to use your ebook, it can make you a very nice sum of money.

Graphic Design Work

This one works if you are a graphic designer or at least do it as a hobby. You can create digital items and designs that can be sold to other people who perhaps don't have the time to do it themselves. Many designers work according to strict deadlines, and that means that they will be looking for elements that will enhance their work but not take up too much time in designing.

Textures, objects, vector icons, and typefaces are all things that can be designed and sold. If you are already a designer, you would probably be creating these types of things while working for your regular clients. So the work would have already been done, and all you need to do is sell what you've got. It is a great way to generate passive income, and it can create leads for you to do freelance work if that is something you want to look into.

Online Courses

People are very interested in learning new skills but don't have a ton of money to spend on new degrees and formal education. That is why the world of online courses is exploding. You can pretty much learn anything online at a fraction of the cost of formal education. If you have some knowledge you want to share or are an expert in something, you could offer this knowledge through an online course.

There are plenty of places where you host your online course. Udemy, Teachable, and Skillshare are among the most popular. The courses on these platforms vary from arts and crafts all the way to accounting. You can make a course about anything that you want to. Some people want to learn a new hobby and others want to advance themselves in their careers by learning a new professional skill.

Some ideas for courses you can create are:

- Singing or dancing
- Yoga

- How to use programs like Excel or even coding programs like Python or .Net
- Tai chi
- Playing musical instruments
- Languages
- Writing
- Public speaking
- Painting
- Cooking

That is just scratching the surface of the types of things that can be taught through an online course. Look at the types of courses on the platforms mentioned above for some inspiration.

<u>Sell Your Music</u>

If you are into music and can play an instrument, you could get paid for doing something that you love. This one is all about the numbers, so you will probably have to put out quite a bit of content before seeing any kind of revenue from it. There are places where you can sell your little jingles, sound effects, and sound clips online. You could also upload your music to music streaming services and get paid as people listen to it.

Whichever one you go for, you will actually have to be good at what you

do. Nobody will want to listen to or use a sound that is awful to listen to. If you don't already have musical talent, then this one may not be for you, although if you are willing to practice and hone your craft, you can definitely go for it. It could be something you do once you have reached financial freedom.

Starting a Side Hustle

All of the above have been focused on doing things to gain passive income, but increasing your income can be done in other ways. The side hustle's art has helped many people increase their income and even quit their jobs. If you can create a passive income, then go for it, but I would like you to know another option. It does require a bit more consistent work, but the amount of money you could be worth it.

The things that have been mentioned in this chapter could be deemed as side hustles. The difference between those and what we will be talking about now is that the passive income hustle's goal is to do something and let it run unattended and make you money. A regular side hustle's goal is to make some extra cash even if you have to do the work consistently.

However, the best side hustles are those you enjoy doing. It becomes a hobby you get paid for, and what's better than that? If you really enjoy your side hustle, you can carry it on into retirement. There is no reason to stop if you really love what you are doing.

Keeping Your Day Job and Starting a Side Hustle

Many people shy away from starting a side hustle because they are worried that it will be too much work or that the quality of work they give to their day job will suffer. I'm not going to lie to you and say that starting a side hustle is easy, but there is no reason you can't have a side hustle and move forward in your career.

You will need to shift your priorities and mindset if you want to make a success of it. Coming home and vegetating on the couch while watching your favorite show on Netflix will be a thing of the past, at least while you are establishing your side hustle and working toward building your portfolio and customer base.

Of course, you should have some balance in your life, but you can't waste your time on things that are not important. Take a look at your schedule and daily activities. If you do not have a schedule, write out a list of everything you do during the day, from dropping the kids off at school to work activities and even your leisure activities.

There will be some things that cannot and should not be removed. These are your everyday work commitments, family commitments, and things that have to do with your health. There might be other things that you deem as very important that you absolutely must have time for. To help you out, highlight and mark all the essential tasks. Everything else that is left would be things that are not that important and can be shifted or completely removed to make room for your side hustle.

There are hundreds of thousands of busy people with side hustles while they have a full-time job. It is absolutely possible; it just takes a mindset shift. You need to be convinced that the side hustle that you are working on is vastly more important than relaxing or working on a hobby (at least for now).

Once you have established yourself, you will again have time to do what you love. A sacrifice now could be the stepping stone you need that will propel you into financial freedom.

Where Do Your Skills Lie and What Are Your Interests?

Chances are that you want to have quick results with this side hustle. To do that, you will have to be good at whatever you are offering or planning to build your side hustle from. You need to be offering something that people want and that you can provide value for. Businesses succeed when the entrepreneur loves what they do and is good at it. It is easier to work toward something and push through hard times when you enjoy what you are doing.

Take some time to go over your skills and see if there is a way to monetize them. If you have music skills, you could give music lessons. If you can edit videos and photos, you could turn that into a side hustle. If you are an accountant, you could do accounting for small businesses and individuals on the side. The possibilities are endless; you just have to find your skill and play to that strength.

If you don't have the skills related to your interest, it is never too late to learn. Develop the necessary skills, and you will be well on your way to building a side hustle that you enjoy doing.

Do Your Research

As with any new business, there will be competition. Unless you have started something completely new that has never been done before, you will have established competitors to go up against. That is why doing your research beforehand is going to be crucial. You need to know what others in your niche are charging and what quality of work customers expect. This research will help you build yourself up and attract customers.

It doesn't matter what your side hustle is about. There will be competitors—if not now, then in a little while when your idea takes off and people want to replicate it. It is all about staying ahead of the game. Research shouldn't just be a one-time thing. There might be something new that pops up in your niche that you could have missed if you are not constantly aware of what is going on in the market.

Pricing will be something that you will have to be competitive with. When you are fairly new, you will need to build credibility before people trust you. To do this, you need customers, and being slightly cheaper than your competitors is a great way to do that at the beginning stages of your side hustle. As you grow, you will be able to increase prices and rework the finances a bit. Just remember that you should not put your prices too low. You will want to make a decent profit for the work you put in.

You should also make sure that the quality of the work you are doing matches and even exceeds that of competitors. Having something to offer that is different from other people in your niche will keep your customers coming back to you and create a draw for new customers. For instance, if you start teaching kids how to play guitar on the side, you could send them home with a video of you coaching them through a song so that they have something to follow along with when they are practicing at home.

Many music schools do not offer this kind of thing, so it could attract people to you and get customers to stay with you. Plus, it would not be that much extra work to create a short tutorial video for them. There will be something a little extra that you could be doing in every niche. It doesn't even have to be something big, and you would be surprised at how small gestures cement relationships and attract people.

Set Clear Goals

Regardless of your side hustle, it will need clearly defined goals to succeed. All side hustles are businesses, and you need to know where you are going with it. The goals that you set have to be attainable and measurable. Very vague goals don't give direction and can be challenging to know when you are making progress. You should dream big but set your goals small.

Instead of setting a goal like "start a successful copywriting business," your goals should be something like "acquire one new customer this month." It allows you to measure if you have met the goal or not, and it doesn't sound like some far-off goal that will take forever to achieve. If your first goal was to get 100 customers, you could very easily get overwhelmed and then not want to move forward with it. However, one customer is doable, and it sets something ahead to be celebrated.

<u>Be Respectful of Your Day Job</u>

In all this, don't forget that you have a day job. You will need to balance your side hustle and your day job for it to all be worth it. Your regular job will be your primary source of income, at least at the beginning of your side hustle, so you need to perform well at it to not get fired. Your side hustle should not take precedence over your usual nine to five unless it has exceeded your regular monthly salary and you want to turn it into your main source of income.

Be aware of your employee agreements so that you do not violate anything while working on the side hustle. You shouldn't use company resources or work on your things during company time. While you are on the clock, you owe it to your company to give it the best you've got.

It is never a good idea to burn bridges. You never know when you will need your employers or coworkers again. If you do something at work that destroys your relationship with them, that could end up biting you in the butt later on. Also, not fulfilling your side of employee agreements could cause a disciplinary hearing or even for the company to take legal action against you, depending on what the infringement was. It's best to avoid this whole situation by being ethical and sticking to the company's rules.

My Side Hustle Is Successful. Should I Quit My Job?

If your side hustle is really doing well and you enjoy the work you are doing, it may be the right time to quit your job and put all of your efforts into your business. Now this decision should not be taken lightly. To be viable for you to leave your job, you need to be sure that you will be financially stable with what you are making through your current side hustle.

When you are thinking about FIRE, you should also weigh whether you will be able to reach your early retirement goals sooner or at the same pace with just the income from the side hustle. You may hate your job at the moment and just want to get out of there, but I would suggest refraining from that until you are absolutely sure.

As a general rule, your side hustle should be making you at least 75% of your annual income that you get from your day job. It will at least cover your expenses but will still make a dent in your savings goals. There is no correct formula here because you could significantly increase your side hustle's earning to twice as much as your day job if you were to give it your full attention. You have to crunch the numbers and feel confident enough to go for it. Some risks are worth taking as long as they have been well thought through.

Whether you are just doing a side hustle to make extra cash to reach your saving goals or want to continue working while doing something you love, a side hustle can be very rewarding. If you love what you do, you can carry it into retirement as an extra income source. The best hobbies are those that can make you some extra money!

Chapter 6

INVEST FOR FINANCIAL FREEDOM

I nvesting is a way to make your money work for you. Just placing it in a savings account or under your mattress is not the best use for your money. Investing is a way of saving your money but receiving more than what you put in. So, yes, you need to save your money, but you also need to invest it to get the best return for it.

You may not see this money coming in immediately. Investing is a long game and relies on the power of compounding. Compounding is when you get interest from the money you put, and then the interest continues to be earned on the new amount. As the amount in your investment account grows, so does the amount of interest you are earning. The more you keep reinvesting, the more your money grows and the quicker it grows.

Assess Your Risk Tolerance

Your risk tolerance changes with age. As you get older or closer to retirement, your risk tolerance will get lower, and you will have to be more conservative to preserve your accumulated finds. The reason is that a market downturn could cripple your retirement plans if it happens close to when you want to retire. The further away you are from retirement, the more risk you can take on because you have more time to recover or to wait out the market.

Dierking (2020) suggests that you subtract your age by 110 to assess your risk tolerance. If you are 70 years old, you should split up your portfolio so that 40% would go to higher risk stocks and 60% would be invested into lower-risk bonds. That is just a general guideline. You also have to consider how you feel about risk and where you are in your retirement journey.

It can be tempting to increase your portfolio risk if you are behind on your savings. High risk does mean that you have a chance for a high reward, but it also means a higher risk of it dropping. Throwing all your eggs in one basket might work on some occasions, but it is clearly not advisable. You can very quickly make the situation worse by taking a high-risk strategy.

Of course, you should have some risk in your portfolio. Playing it too safe means that there is slower growth. If you are more risk-tolerant and want to go for it, start by increasing it by 10% and see where it goes rather than going all in. This way, you still have some conservative savings but can also profit off a high-risk portfolio.

Diversify Your Investments

Placing all of your money into one place could be disastrous for your retirement. The truth is that we never really know what is going to happen in the future, and the market can be very unpredictable. If you have everything placed in stocks, you will be forced to sell at a loss if it all goes down.

Your investment portfolio should be as diversified as possible. If there is a downturn, you will have enough to lessen the damage and be able to ride it out until it pickles up again. As stated earlier, your portfolio should have some risk, but you should have some income sources that aren't as exposed to market risk. Examples of these are bonds with staggered maturity dates or a bond ladder. If you have this, you will have enough cash at the ready, in a high-yield savings account, so it can carry you through, and you won't have to sell your investments at a loss. Timing the market is very difficult, so there is no exact formula of when you should pull out your money. Sometimes you will miss the mark and have to wait it out until your investments go back up. It pays to be prepared for this because the longer you can wait, the better for your investment. Investors usually advise that you stay in the market for longer periods. Having a diversified investment portfolio allows you to have the freedom to wait it out when you need to. It prevents you from pulling out your investments at a loss if that scenario does happen.

Are There Other Types of Investing?

Stocks and bonds are not the only options when it comes to investing. You can also get into investing in real estate. That is completely different from investing in stocks since it has different risks and challenges, but also different benefits and rewards. Under the right circumstances, investing in property can be a viable substitution for stocks. It can offer lower risk, provide more diversification, and yield better returns. When you buy real estate, you are buying a physical piece of land or property. Your returns are gained from rent and through appreciation since property values go up. Many people find property investing attractive because they buy a tangible asset that can be controlled. When you buy a stock, you buy a piece of the company, but it is not tangible in the sense that you can go in and make changes—unless you own a significant amount of the company, and this is generally not the case. However, you can similarly invest in real estate as you would in stocks through REITs or real estate investment trusts.

Whether you invest in real estate or stocks is a personal choice. It also depends on your investment style, goals, and financial situation. If you can do both, that would create greater diversification in your investment portfolio. There are risks involved with both of them. Any time you invest your money, there is a chance that you might lose it or only increase your initial investment by a small margin. However, investing is worth it because it offers a higher reward than regular savings accounts. If you are unsure about where you want to invest, let's look at each choice's pros and cons.

Real Estate Investing

Let's first talk about the pros and cons of real estate investing. Owning property has probably been the goal of the vast majority of people. Now is the time to weigh up your options and determine if it is the best option for you.

Pros of Real Estate Investing

The first pro of real estate investing is that it is reasonably easy to understand. All you have to do is buy a property, maintain it, and collect rent if you choose to rent it out. The other way you can make money from property is to buy it and flip it for a profit. Even just living in the house and waiting for the value to increase before selling it is a return on investment.

Real estate also provides a form of passive income. If you are renting out your property, you will be getting money in your bank account every month. It also feels more secure because if something were to go wrong and you lose a large chunk of your money or income, at least you will have a place to live and a tangible asset on your books.

Another positive of real estate is that you can invest even when you do not have the full amount to do so. You will most likely be taking out a mortgage to finance the property. You will then only need a down payment of about 20% for you to own the property. If you were going to rent out the property, the rent could pay off the rest of the mortgage while getting some sort of passive income.

Owning a home or property means that you may qualify for some tax benefits. You may be able to get a tax deduction on mortgage interest up to about the first $1 million in mortgage debt. There are also scenarios where you could avoid capital gains and get some tax breaks.

Cons of Real Estate Investing

There are a few cons to real estate investing, the obvious one being that it is more work than investing in stocks. When you own a property or a house, it is your job to ensure that it is taken care of and that maintenance is up to date. That is especially important if you have a rental property. You are a landlord, and wherever there is a problem, you are the person the tenants will call. There is a lot more physical work required when it comes to owning a property.

Even though you do not have to pay all the money upfront, you will still need quite a large sum of money to start investing in property. If you plan to buy a property valued at $250,000, the down payment you would need to secure it would be $50,000, which is 20% of the price. You might even want to put down a larger down payment so that you can lower the monthly repayments on the house. Either way, it is quite a sizable amount to be put down right off the bat.

If you want to get your money out of the real estate, it can be quite a lengthy process. The money is not as liquid as it is with stocks. You will have to go through the process of selling your house, and there is no exact timeline to how long this will take. It is a process that will take some patience since you do not want to sell to the first person that makes an offer if the offer is lower than what you initially wanted.

The property game is all about location. One location can skyrocket in value, and another can hit a slump. That is due to many different factors like development in the area or even political uncertainty or general safety. Most of the time, this cannot be predicted, so it is a good idea to diversify your property by location and type. It means having various properties in different areas and having both commercial and residential properties. It is complicated to diversify your income if you do not have deep pockets and a large amount of money to invest in all of these properties. It is pretty much impossible for the average investor to do this, at least at the beginning of building wealth.

Investing in Stocks

Investing in the stock market is probably the first thing people think of when the word 'investing' comes up. Just like most things in life, there are pros and cons. Take a look at them and decide whether investing in stocks is the best move for you.

<u>Pros of Investing in Stocks</u>

Stocks are quite different from real estate in many ways. One of these is the fact that stocks are highly liquid, meaning you can take out your money and move it around whenever you like. If you decide to remove your money from the market, all it takes is a few clicks. You will always know your stocks' value because the numbers are available for you to see right on your screen.

It is also quite easy to diversify your investments when dealing with stocks. You can invest in various companies in different sectors and industries with little effort. In fact, you can do this through mutual funds or index funds. These buy shares in multiple different companies and give their investors instant diversification.

Another advantage is that you can grow your money in a tax-advantaged retirement account, like a 401(k). When you purchase shares through a retirement account, you can let your account grow tax-free or tax-deferred. It will add a little extra cash to your investment portfolio.

<u>Cons of Investing in Stocks</u>

Unfortunately, stock prices can be quite volatile. They are not as stable as real estate. You will see stock prices moving up and down at quite a fast pace. If you are not playing the long game where you buy and hold your shares until you see it peaking up high, it can be very difficult to watch. This type of volatility makes people want to remove their money from the market prematurely. You may have to pay capital gains tax when you sell your stocks. However, if you have held onto your stock for at least a year, you may qualify for some reductions on this. There might also be taxes to be paid on any stock dividends paid out to you throughout the year.

Often people struggle with stocks because the volatility triggers emotional decision making. It is easy to sell and buy stocks that people will just do it at a whim instead of sitting back and thinking about it. The market wavering is a big trigger for investors, and they end up selling their stocks when they should have held them for longer. In most cases, it is better to buy and hold your stocks for as long as possible; this is the best way to get the most out of your investments. Taking a long view is the best way to build up any investment portfolio.

Financial education

When we think about improving our financial condition, we usually focus on quick ways to get rich. It's all about making as much money as possible in the quickest length of time.

These types of ideas and methods, however, do not work for the majority of people. Typically, you must already have a reasonable amount of money saved and be willing to invest it and risk losing it. A good financial future, like many other things, needs time, patience, and some
education. I understand that this may not be what you want to hear, but let me explain why financial literacy is the most critical step on your path to financial wealth.

For a long time, many consumers have had little understanding of finances, how credit works, and the potential impact on financial well-being that poor financial decisions can cause. Indeed, a lack of financial knowledge has been identified as one of the primary reasons why many Americans struggle with saving and investing.

What Exactly Is Financial Literacy?

Financial literacy is the integration of financial, credit, and debt management knowledge required to make financially responsible decisions—choices that are essential in our daily lives. Knowing how a checking account works, what using a credit card truly means, and how to prevent debt are all examples of this knowledge.

To summarize, financial literacy has a tangible influence on families as they attempt to balance their budgets, purchase a home, support their children's education, and assure a retirement income.

Although financial literacy varies with education and income, evidence suggests that highly educated customers with high incomes can be just as clueless about financial concerns as less-educated, lower-income people (although, in general, the latter tend to be less financially literate). Furthermore, consumers regard financial decision-making and education as complicated and anxiety-inducing.

Why financial literacy matters

Many people feel that financial planning is only for the wealthy, or at least the accountants who work for the wealthy. However, regardless of socioeconomic level, financial literacy and education are critical skills that everyone should begin cultivating at an early age. The more familiar you are with the financial world, the more steady you will be in life.

There is an increasing demand for financial education

Individuals must be able to grasp their financial status and make informed decisions now more than ever. As people struggle to stay up with the financial world, various causes make financial literacy a more critical ability.

Because people live longer lives, retirees will need more savings than earlier generations to maintain the same degree of comfort and financial stability.

The financial landscape is growing increasingly complex. Banks, credit unions, insurance firms, credit card companies, mortgage companies, and other financial service companies all compete for consumers' attention, adding to the confusion caused by the number of complex investment and savings products.

Government assistance is no longer adequate. Whereas past generations relied on Social Security monies during their retirement, the Social Security Trust Fund is expected to be totally exhausted by 2033. Most folks will not have enough savings to last their entire lifetimes if they do not plan ahead of time.

Income and financial literacy

Brown University professors analyzed information from various financial literacy studies, including a literacy survey that asked five fundamental financial questions to respondents of varying ages and experience levels. The data analysis generated some surprising but not unexpected outcomes. For example, only 5% of people between the ages of 18 and 24 correctly answered all financial literacy questions. However, comprehension appeared to improve with age, as 19% of those aged 65 and up aced the test.

The most important factor, however, seems to be household income. Twelve percent of persons earning $35,000 to $49,000 answered each question correctly, while 37 percent of those earning $150,000 or more achieved a perfect score. While more money does not guarantee greater financial literacy, it is reasonable to presume that those who are more economically successful have more financial education and practice.

Chapter 7

REDESIGN YOUR LIFESTYLE

B eing a part of the FIRE movement does mean there will be a shift in your lifestyle. This change will be both during the time you are saving and when you choose to retire. You will have to make these changes to sustain yourself throughout retirement. FIRE is not for those who are unwilling to make the necessary changes.

For most people who want to retire early, it will mean that they will have to choose a similar lifestyle to what their peers are currently living with. Resisting temptation and focusing on why you are doing this will be key to your success. There is no greater reward than being financially free and not having to worry about making ends meet or being stressed out at a job you hate. That is the main goal, not to be rich but to be free.

With this in mind, let's go through some of the major lifestyle changes you will have to make when deciding to go on the FIRE journey. All of these will apply unless you are an extremely high earner and can afford a similar lifestyle while still saving a lot of money. Also, if you are working toward fatFIRE, some of these will not apply to you when you have reached fatFIRE as you will be increasing your standard of living by quite a bit once you retire.

Changing Your Relationship With Money

Working toward FIRE means changing your relationship with money. To be happy, you need to have a healthy view of what money actually is. Managing your money well requires you to have the right view on money and take the right steps.

Managing your money well will be one of the things that allow you to stay happy and financially free for the rest of your life.

<u>Educate Yourself About Money</u>

Being educated about money and how it works will allow you to make better financial decisions moving forward. It is not only about knowing how to save but also about making your money work for you. Continuously increasing your financial intelligence will help you not get caught off guard in the future.

You can get some valuable tips and tricks when you are continuously learning.

This financial education does not have to come from any formal course. You can learn a lot by subscribing to financial podcasts and following blogs that post about money. It is a quick way to feed yourself information, and it does not cost you a thing. If you can do a course, I would advise that you do. Even a short one on Udemy or another online course website could change the way you view and handle money. Books and videos are also great tools to further your knowledge. It is not about becoming a financial guru but rather about putting yourself in the best position to make the right decisions when you need to.

Personal financial education is not something that is taught to us in school or university, so we have to take it upon ourselves to learn and grow.

Learn to Ask for Help

If you are confused about something or need help with making a financial decision, don't be afraid to ask. Have someone around you who you can trust and can go to when you are not sure about something regarding your finances. Money does not have to be a taboo subject. I know that it is not often discussed, but how will we learn if we never talk about it and ask for the information we need?

We can learn a lot from other people's situations. You don't have to lay out your entire financial history in front of your friends, but make sure that there is someone you can go to. It can be a spouse, parent, sibling, or friend. It is even better if you have a financial advisor. They are there to assist you, so don't feel shy to ask.

Schedule a Money Date

Setting a date for when you will sit down and go through your finances is so important. If you do this every week or every month, you will know that you have a handle on your money. That is essential when you are saving toward retirement, but it is even more important when you have retired and are relying on your savings to pay your salary.

You need to know where your money is going, how much you are saving, and if there is anything you spent your money unnecessarily when you are saving toward retirement. If you are not aware of these things, you could think you are closer to your goal than you actually are. If that is the case, you can develop a plan of action and do a quick course correction. It is also good for your motivation to keep track of your progress. Seeing that you keep getting closer to your goals will be a continuous motivation source for you.

When you have retired, this money date will give you peace of mind that you are still within your limits and will have enough for the rest of your life. If you notice something is off or that you have spent a little more than you should have, you can recalculate and fix the problem. This kind of course correction is vital fo. you when you are no longer working.

Setting a specific day when you will go through all your financial statements and transactions makes you accountable to yourself, and it gets you into the habit of checking up on yourself. It's not about being pedantic about your money, but just being aware of what is going on. As any human relationship needs attention, your relationship with money also needs to be prioritized.

Always Remember the Basics

The more you educate yourself about money, the easier it might be to forget about the basics. The basics are what your financial freedom is built on, and it is what will keep your foundation strong. There will be many opinions and new ideas out there, but you have to use a filter when you are listening to them.

Just because there seems to be some new way to invest or a new method to increase the amount of money you have, does not mean you have to follow it. As long as you have your foundations right, you will be okay. Here are the basic principles you need to keep in your mind at all times when you are dealing with money:

- Spend less than what you earn.
- Invest and make your money work for you.
- Make sure you have a plan for your money and stick to it.

These principles have been mentioned in some form throughout this book. If you keep them close and stick to them, you will be in a better financial position than most Americans.

Being Fulfilled by What Really Matters

We live in a world obsessed with the bigger, better, and fancier.

Everyone is trying to buy the best thing to show off, and it can be easy to fall into that trap. The thing is that all of those things are not the most important things. When you speak to millionaires, big entrepreneurs, and CEOs, they do not wish they had made more money or bought more of the coolest stuff. They wish they had spent more time with their families, learned more, and focused on doing the things they genuinely love.

Spending your life just to make money is a worthless pursuit because money truly cannot buy happiness. That is why most of the FIRE movement is not about making a whole bunch of money so that you can live this grand life. It is about having enough freedom to do the things that fulfill you.

Most people who have reached FIRE live pretty simple lives, but they are pleased because they are not controlled by the need to have more stuff and live a life outside of their means. It is okay to have a simple and authentic life, one that is filled with you spending your time doing things you care about.

When you do a Google search for "how to have a fulfilled life," you will notice that there are hardly any results that show anything to do with having more stuff or living an extravagant life. That is because in the grand scheme of life, those things do not really matter.

Regardless of where you find the advice for reaching fulfillment, they all have the same three recurring things. These are to spend your time wisely, focus on building healthy relationships, and give back generously. These three things seem to be the cornerstone of a fulfilled life. There will be other things that help you feel fulfilled and add value to your life, but if you were to just focus on these three, your life quality would significantly improve.

As we already know, time is our most important resource. It is also a finite resource, which means that we cannot get it back once it is done, and there is no replacement for it. That alone should help you realize how important it is to spend your time on the right things. Where you spend your time will determine your life's direction and shape who you are.

Spending time with people and things that grow you and make you a better person is needed if you want to live a fulfilled life. If you want to know if you are spending your time in the right places, make a list of everything you spent your time on in the day. If you notice that you spent a lot of time on things that were draining, unnecessary, or just made you outright unhappy, then it may be time for a shift.

We are social creatures; there is no way to get around that. Even the quietest, introverted person needs to have other people in their life. Even though social interaction is a need, it can also be draining if we surround ourselves with the wrong people. People who are unhappy, unsupportive, and just negative are not the types of people you should be fostering relationships with. Family and friends who love you and who you have close ties with should be your main priority. These are the relationships that feed your soul. Life is so much better when you have the right people around.

The last area that can make your life fulfilling is giving back generously. Being generous is not something that comes naturally to many of us. I would even go as far as to say that we are naturally selfish. All you have to do is look at a toddler with a new toy. If they don't hold on tight and say "Mine!" when you ask for it, I would be very surprised. Just because this is a default does not make it right. The most fulfilled people are the ones that are generous and care for others.

Now, you don't only have to be generous with your money. You can give your time, which, as we have discussed, is our most precious resource. Just doing something for someone else and lending a helping hand improves our mood and makes us more grateful for our things. It gives us a perspective shift that we so often need. It may come back to the fact that we are social beings and need that sense of community. Community is giving to those that need it and helping where you can.

Be Social but Be Smart

Common culture states that you have to spend money to have a social life. It is the norm, but it does not have to be true. No rule says that you have to spend a bucket load of money to go out and have fun. It is just the consumerism mindset.

Let's admit it, food and drinks are where we spend most when going out. A simple dinner and drinks can end up breaking the bank, and you don't really have anything to show for it. Thankfully, you can do a few things to make your social events less expensive and save some money in the process.

Order Smarter

As mentioned above, food and drinks can leave your wallet dry after a night out. Sometimes you can't avoid going out to get food with your friends, but it still doesn't mean that you have to overspend. Making a few simple ordering swaps will help you keep your spending to a minimum.

Firstly, if it is possible to avoid dinner, then do it. Dinner is far more expensive than breakfast, brunch, or lunch. If you just look at a restaurant's menu, you will see the price difference between the dinner menu and any other meal. Not only that, but it is much easier to overspend at dinner than it is at any other meal.

Whether you are out for dinner or brunch, be aware of the prices of the items you are ordering. There will always be something cheaper on the menu that you can order. Even ordering an appetizer for a meal is a great hack. Most of the time, the appetizers are a decent size, so you will still leave the restaurant full. If you know you will still be hungry when you do this, then eat something before you go out so that you aren't tempted to order something huge.

Lastly, be aware of drinks. These are the silent killers of your bank balance. Drinks are where restaurants make their money since they are often very overpriced. It goes for both alcoholic drinks and regular soft drinks. If you are going out for a night of drinks, suggest that you do pre-drinks at home to not have to spend so much on cocktails or beers. If you are at a restaurant, stick to water. Maybe have one drink, and then the rest of the night order water. Your bill at the end of the night will be significantly cheaper.

<u>Take Advantage of Free Events and Activities</u>

There are plenty of free and low-cost things to do as a group if you look for them. Friends just need an excuse to hang out with each other; they do not need something that costs a lot of money. Often we spend all that money on social events because we do not know that there is another option.

Some things that you could consider doing are having a picnic at a park, having a games night, hosting a potluck, going hiking, or going on a bike ride. No matter where you live, all of these things should be possible. There will probably be lots of cheap or free things to do in your city or town as well. Look out for park concerts with a very low entrance fee or free because they allow up-and-coming artists to play. Art events also tend to have a cheap admission ticket, if any. Farmers' markets are also great for walking around and having a relaxed afternoon.

All you have to do is get a little creative or research to find out what is available in your area. You are probably surrounded by very low-cost entertainment forms that are yet to be discovered.

Take Control

If you are the one who gets in front of the planning, you can steer it in the direction you want it. You can suggest less expensive activities like bike riding or hiking. Getting in front of the planning is one of the best things you can do because it saves you from saying no when your friends suggest something expensive.

The chances are that you will have friends that are not into FIRE, and that can make going out harder. You would want to be thrifty, and they still want to spend all their money. You still want to hang out with them, but it just has to be on different terms than it used to be. It helps to be honest with your friends and tell them that you are not keen on doing expensive things anymore and want to be a bit more frugal.

If you show them all the fun things you guys could be doing without spending large amounts of money, they will probably get on board. Most of the time, your friends and social circle will just want to hang out. That is essentially what dinner and drinks are—an excuse to get together. There are plenty of other ways to meet this end; you just have to show them that it is possible to do so.

Just Say No

There will probably be times when you will have to say no to family and friends' social events. If it is really going to blow your budget and cause you to spend money that you don't want to, it is okay to say no. You don't have to be present for every single social gathering. As long as it is not an extremely important event, your friends and family will have no right to be upset.

Usually, if you say that you do not have the money for it this month, they will drop it. It is a valid excuse, and nobody can fault another for giving a social event a skip for financial reasons. You will get the chance to hang out with them again. If you have explained to them that you are on a journey to financial freedom, they will probably expect you to not attend to certain things.

You Will Have to Deal With Criticism

Whenever someone tries something that is not the norm, they are bound to face some sort of criticism. If this happens to you, think about what you are working toward. Keep focused and try to brush it off. The truth is that not everyone will understand why you are doing what you are doing. Some people might even get offended that you cannot go out like you used to, but you have to remember that you are doing this for yourself and not for other people.

People will criticize what they do not understand. Some will not want to understand. If you are faced with someone like this, it is best not to try to explain yourself. You will get nowhere and end up frustrated. It is tough when close friends and family criticize or make fun of you, but eventually, you will have something to show for it, and they will have nothing more to say. It is not as easy as just cutting people off who disagree with how you choose to live your life. Unless it is a very extreme situation, there will be no need to completely cut anybody off.

Instead, be prepared for the criticism and try to distance yourself to get a break from them. There is no shame in not wanting to keep putting yourself in those types of situations, but do your best to keep your relationships. Once people start to realize that you are serious about FIRE and a lifestyle change, they will back off.

Finding FIRE Friends

There is nothing wrong if you want to keep your old friends, but it obviously helps if you have some friends who are on the same journey as you are. This way, you will have people to share ideas with, who understand where you are coming from. It's not that your old friends are bad or that you have to ditch them, but the truth is that they will probably not understand why you are doing what you are doing, so they will never be able to support you in the way that you might need.

Finding people who are pursuing the same goals as you will make the journey more comfortable and a lot more fun. It might be difficult to find people on the FIRE journey since it is not like a telltale sign that someone is part of the movement. The easiest way to find like-minded people will be on online groups. A large subreddit is just dedicated to FIRE, where supporters share their ideas, triumphs, and struggles.

There are also Facebook groups and Instagram pages that you can follow or join. It is easier to connect with people on a social media group, and hopefully you will be able to find someone who lives close to you. Certain groups might also host events, conferences, and meetups where you could meet people who are all part of the FIRE movement.

Try as many things as you can so that you will get the right people around you. Life is much better when you have the right people around you.

Chapter 8

AFTER RETIREMENT

Y ou made it! You have saved and worked hard to get to this point, but now what? Sometimes, when you plan so long for something, it seems weird when you get there, and you may even feel a little lost. Don't worry. There have been many people in your shoes, and that feeling is only temporary. You are doing a complete change of lifestyle, so there is bound to be some settling-in that needs to happen. Before you get to the FIRE retirement stage, try to prepare your mind for the switch.

Managing Your Finances When You Retire

Unfortunately, you won't be able to just put your finances on cruise mode when you retire. You will still have to manage your money correctly to make sure that it lasts for the rest of your life. If you do not do this, you could risk running out of money and having to get a job to support you, or you might just have to live on a measly amount every month. Neither of these situations are ideal, so let's just make sure that you know what you need to be doing by the time you get to retirement.

Create Spending Guidelines

A lot of people mess up when it comes to retirement because they blow most of their money in the first few years. That leaves them with a minimal amount to live off for the rest of their retirement. Remember that while it may seem you got a lot of money in the bank, this is meant to last you for the rest of your life.

The best thing you can do is set guardrails for yourself. These will tell you what you are allowed to spend in the month without risking using up all your money. Create three guardrails: the lower, middle, and higher-end guardrails.

The lower guardrail will show you the minimum amount of money you will be able to spend and still survive. If you spend the bare minimum, it will be just what you need to cover your expenses and not account for anything fun or lavish. The middle guardrail will be a more realistic budget because it covers expenses and does allow for a bit of fun money and small amounts of unexpected spending. The higher guardrail will be the maximum amount you will be able to spend while still staying safely within your budget.

Most of the time, you should be staying in the middle, but this type of budgeting will allow you to see how much wiggle room you have. You will have less anxiety about spending because you know that there are a maximum and minimum you can go while still being safe. It will also allow you to enjoy your retirement and splurge a little on experiences and things you truly value.

Chances are every month will not look the same, so you won't be able to spend the exact same. You also don't want to live a so financially lean life that you cannot do anything enjoyable for fear of running out of money. Sitting down every month and creating a budget for yourself will also help allocate your spending. You are probably doing this now (and if not, then you should start), but this should carry on into retirement.

Now you are getting a monthly salary from your employer; when you retire, you will be getting your 'salary' from your savings. That is the only difference. You still need to be wise about where you spend your money, especially if you are not planning on doing something similar to fatFIRE.

<u>Consider Having a Source of Income</u>

Having a source of income is a great way to feel like you are stable. Although you will have planned to have enough money throughout retirement, sometimes we all need that little extra cushion of security. You can take your time to figure out what you want to do and how you would like to make money because you will have unlimited time once you have retired.

Trying to create a passive stream of income is a great option. Investing in property, writing books or music, or creating an online course are great ways to create some passive income after doing the initial work. It also gives you something to work toward if you feel that being a retiree is getting a bit boring. Use what you are good at or your passions to try to make some extra cash on the side.

Wait as Long as You Can Before Accessing Social Security

There is something to consider later on in your retirement years. You can start collecting Social Security from the age of 62, but it is worth it to hold off on this for as long as you can. The sooner you start with Social Security, the less money you will get. In fact, the difference can be up to hundreds of thousands of dollars.

The earliest you can get Social Security is 62, and the latest is 70. If you can push for the oldest possible age, then you should do so. If you absolutely must take it out, then, of course, go ahead, but waiting is undoubtedly the better option. You will be able to enjoy a higher standard of living in those final years.

Take Care of Your Health

As we get older, our health often deteriorates. It seems like the normal progression of life, but it does not have to be this way. Some things are out of our control, like if we get diagnosed with a chronic illness, but most of our health is in our hands. By taking care of yourself, you are setting yourself up for a great retirement all the way up into the later stages of life. Health problems can be costly, and you want to spend your money on things you will enjoy rather than doctors' bills.

Making sure that your health is taken care of will also add a few years to your life and allow you to live a full, active life for as long as possible. Exercise and eating healthy should always be a priority. Choose to eat a balanced diet packed with the nutrients that your body needs. I know people do not like exercising, but you do not have to do something you hate.

Getting your body active with just a simple 30-minute walk or doing a sport that you enjoy has a world of health benefits. We hear many big names in finance and business ranting about how important it is to prioritize health and wellbeing. So it is definitely not just for models and social media influencers. You will thank yourself later on in life if you make an effort to take care of your body now.

Keep Assessing and Planning

If you want to make sure that you are always on the right track, you will need to keep assessing where you are and make the necessary adjustments. As I mentioned earlier, setting your finances on cruise control will not work. Life is unpredictable, so no formula can be put in place to ensure that everything runs smoothly. Keep checking in with your finances and see if you are still in a good space.

Things like your investments' performance and a shift in priorities could mean that you have to change your original plan to accommodate it. It doesn't mean that all of the planning that you have done in the past has become null and void.

The plans you have made give you a solid base, and everything else will probably not require as much work. Usually, it is just small shifts and shuffles. As long as you remember to check in with yourself and allow for some changes, you will be able to enjoy your retirement in a variety of different circumstances and situations.

Retired Does Not Mean Never Working or Learning

Some people can retire at age 40 and live a leisurely life with nothing to do. If you are one of those people and that is your goal, don't let anyone stop you from doing that. However, that is a very small group of people. Most people think they want to relax and do nothing for the rest of their life, but a year or even a couple of months in, they find themselves frustrated or bored.

You should remember that just because you're retired and do not have to work for your living does not mean that you don't have to work at all. You can still work, whether for money or just for fun. You will need something to occupy your time and keep your mind active. Even having an intense hobby can help you out. You are free to pick any kind of work you want. If you want to landscape, go ahead. If you want to renovate, feel free. If you want to start a new business venture, nothing is stopping you.

The beauty of financial freedom is that nothing prevents you from chasing your dreams. You have all the time in the world, and you are financially taken care of. You can spend your free time working on building something you are really passionate about. If you need extra money to fund your venture, you have the time to raise it by whatever means necessary.

Try not to fall into the trap of complacency. You should still be keeping active and setting goals for yourself to reach. Being completely sedentary and not giving your mind the stimulation it needs could have a negative impact on your health. You do not want to have your life cut short due to health complications. There is plenty to do out there, even if you do not want to work for money. Take some courses, learn a new skill, or make something. It can be fulfilling and will keep your brain and body active.

Enjoy Your Retirement

Once you retire, it is time to enjoy your wealth. You worked hard for it. Of course, this is not permission to blow every dollar you can, but you can't be scared to spend your money. You have done all the hard work and planning at the point of retirement, so you need to trust that it is okay to spend.

Many people who save aggressively struggle to make the switch to spending. They have saved and cut expenses so much that it is just what they have become used to. Remember the extreme saving is only temporary, so when it is time to spend, you need to be able to let go of the reins a little and enjoy the fruit of your labor.

That is why creating a budget and spending plan is worth the effort. You will know what you have to spend, so you will not feel guilty or anxious about it. Life is about experiences and doing what you love most. Now that you have made the sacrifices necessary to get there quickly, it is time to really live the life you have been working so hard to achieve.

You are never too young to find life satisfaction. Life is meant to be enjoyed and experienced the way you want to. It is so sad that some people will work so hard their whole lives to retire only when they are too old to enjoy their retirement. I think of senior cruises, and I think it is a waste because the people who go are too old to enjoy everything the cruise offers.

orkeling, swimming, visiting the islands when the docks. These are the best parts of a cruise, but if re too old or tired to even get off the ship, you ake the most of this experience.

That is why it is important not to wait until later and use every moment you have to live the best version of your life. Financial independence allows you to be free to live the life you desire and create the memories you want to. It is not even about being retired and having a relaxing time for the rest of your life. It is about releasing yourself to be fulfilled in every area of your life and allowing yourself to find the part of life that makes life worth living. Now that you have reached financial independence, you should make the most of it.

CONCLUSION

Y ou have just finished reading this book, and your head is probably swimming just thinking about how you are going to get started on your FIRE journey. May I just suggest that you start with the simple things first? Assess where you stand financially. Lay it all out on the table. It may be challenging to acknowledge that you are not where you want to be. Perhaps you will find that you are in better shape than you thought you were. Whichever category you are in, at least you have a good idea of your starting point. From this point, you can start planning.

The central premise of the FIRE model is to save aggressively. You do this in any way you can to get to your goal of financial independence quicker. By now, you know that it is not an easy task. It will take some sacrifice and some reshuffling of priorities, but it is so worth it. Ward off that need for instant gratification so that you can have the sweet satisfaction of not being bound by someone else's agenda just because they are paying you.

Wherever you start, just know that you can reach your financial independence goal. You can make a life for yourself that you deem worth living. It is definitely attainable with a little bit of elbow grease and the right plan of action. Find your motivation, find your momentum, and get going. You can get started today and just keep moving forward. You will be so glad you did when you finally reach FIRE!

"If you want to be financially free, you need to become a different person than you are today and let go of whatever has held you back in the past." - **Robert Kiyosaki**

CPSIA information can be obtained
at www.ICGtesting.com
Printed in the USA
LVHW082253120323
741470LV00001B/218

9 781915 218209